CAMBRIDGE LIP~ ^~~~

Books of endi

H

The books reissued in this series inc
movements by eye-witnesses and co.   , ... as landmark
studies that assembled significant source materials or developed new
historiographical methods. The series includes work in social, political and
military history on a wide range of periods and regions, giving modern
scholars ready access to influential publications of the past.

General Gordon's Letters
from the Crimea, the Danube and Armenia

This volume of letters was published in 1884, when General Gordon
(1833–85) was engaged in the controversial defence of Khartoum that
claimed his life the following year. The reputation of 'Chinese' Gordon, a
complex figure, unpopular with the British government and military but
adored by the people and press, was fed by works such as this. Covering his
time in the Crimea as a young lieutenant, and later in the drawing up
of the new frontiers between the Russian and Ottoman empires, these letters
were published by his later biographer, Demetrius C. Boulger (1853–1928)
as evidence of Gordon's strength of character and value as a military leader.
One reviewer noted in them an 'indomitable cheerfulness of disposition,
patient endurance, trustful fatalism, simple courage and faith, ... [and]
single-hearted devotion to duty', words which reflected the popular view
of Gordon as a symbol of British national pride and imperial honour.

Cambridge University Press has long been a pioneer in the reissuing of out-of-print titles from its own backlist, producing digital reprints of books that are still sought after by scholars and students but could not be reprinted economically using traditional technology. The Cambridge Library Collection extends this activity to a wider range of books which are still of importance to researchers and professionals, either for the source material they contain, or as landmarks in the history of their academic discipline.

Drawing from the world-renowned collections in the Cambridge University Library and other partner libraries, and guided by the advice of experts in each subject area, Cambridge University Press is using state-of-the-art scanning machines in its own Printing House to capture the content of each book selected for inclusion. The files are processed to give a consistently clear, crisp image, and the books finished to the high quality standard for which the Press is recognised around the world. The latest print-on-demand technology ensures that the books will remain available indefinitely, and that orders for single or multiple copies can quickly be supplied.

The Cambridge Library Collection brings back to life books of enduring scholarly value (including out-of-copyright works originally issued by other publishers) across a wide range of disciplines in the humanities and social sciences and in science and technology.

General Gordon's Letters from the Crimea, the Danube and Armenia

August 18, 1854, to November 17, 1858

EDITED BY DEMETRIUS C. BOULGER

CAMBRIDGE
UNIVERSITY PRESS

CAMBRIDGE UNIVERSITY PRESS

Cambridge, New York, Melbourne, Madrid, Cape Town,
Singapore, São Paolo, Delhi, Mexico City

Published in the United States of America by Cambridge University Press, New York

www.cambridge.org
Information on this title: www.cambridge.org/9781108044776

This edition first published 1884
This digitally printed version 2012

ISBN 978-1-108-04477-6 Paperback

GENERAL GORDON'S LETTERS

FROM THE CRIMEA, ETC.

GENERAL GORDON'S LETTERS

FROM

THE CRIMEA, THE DANUBE, AND ARMENIA.

AUGUST 18, 1854, TO NOVEMBER 17, 1858.

EDITED BY

DEMETRIUS C. BOULGER,

AUTHOR OF "THE HISTORY OF CHINA," ETC., ETC.

LONDON: CHAPMAN AND HALL,

LIMITED.

1884.

INTRODUCTION.

THE following letters represent the earliest correspondence of General Gordon with members of his family after the commencement of his military career in the service of the Queen. In point of time, it is not probable that they will ever be superseded. When the first note was written from Pembroke Dock he was only a few months over twenty-one; when the last letter was sent from Constantinople he was still two months short of his twenty-sixth birthday. During that period of four years and a half he was constantly employed, with one interval, in connection with events of dramatic character, and the correspondence covers the whole of an epoch important in history and famous in our national annals.

There is a certain appropriateness as well as use
in supplying fuller details of the first part of a
public career which was destined to reveal so
many picturesque and heroic incidents; and those
details cannot be supplied in a clearer or more ample
mannèr thaǹ in the young engineer officer's own
words, though they were set down in all the haste
and weariness of bodily exertion and mental
fatigue in the trenches of the Crimea, amid the
innumerable difficulties and annoyances of rapid
travel in such a region as the Danubian principalities were and still are, and on the desert
heights of the Armenian border lands. The reader
can feel sure that he receives the impression as it
took form under the pen of General Gordon; and
although there is never a pretension to style, the
language is always clear and direct, and no one
can doubt that the writer reveals his true mind.

These letters are not without their use also.
When General Gordon arrived in the Crimea, in
the first days of the year 1855, the more striking
events of the campaign had taken place. The
thin red line had carried the heights of Alma,
the immortal charge of the light brigade had

vindicated the reputation of at least English cavalry, and the attempted surprise of the position of Inkerman had resulted in the rout of the Russians. The winter troubles were in full progress. General Gordon himself was one of the arrivals from England destined to convert those troubles into the hopes of the spring, the waning expectations of the summer, and the long-anticipated triumph of the early autumn. The Historian has duly recorded and described the progress of events up to the period at which General Gordon's Crimean experiences began ; but he has not yet reached that point at which the narrative of events to be found in the following pages really commences. They have, therefore, an intrinsic value apart from that given them by the name of their author. The letters from the Danube and Armenia, which will perhaps be considered the more interesting, are important as giving us from the best possible source the particulars of those two frontier commissions which by the energy of the English Government alone did impose limits for a time to the encroachments of Russia by compelling the Czar to relax his hold on a cherished province in one continent, and on conquered fortresses in another.

But I think the general agreement of the reader will be with me when I say that their greatest importance is that they throw another light on the character of the man who, in the midst of innumerable tokens that an English Government fears its responsibilities, and shrinks with a craven spirit from discharging its part as the exponent of the tradition and mission of England, is affording by his courage and devotion to duty a much needed proof that Englishmen are not yet given over to the cruel and cowardly persuasion that they have but to enunciate some fine moral principle, or to demonstrate their logical consistency as political partisans, in order to escape the guilt of having produced unnecessary rebellion and useless slaughter by a course of action which has for four years put off the decision until the morrow which is always too late. In these pages may be seen the clearness of vision, the promptitude of resolve and action, the steadfast courage, the unswerving devotion to duty, the implicit belief in his own country, which, if remarkable when combined in the person of an individual, are still the essential attributes of a people which as an insignificant minority is charged with and has accepted the task of spreading good government and maintaining peace throughout a great part of the Eastern world.

The man of action is revealed in these letters to his nearest and most intimate relations, recalling what he has said elsewhere, " inaction is terrible to me." There is little also of that religious fervour which has displayed itself in his more recent writings, although it is clear throughout that he is of a serious turn of mind, and not perhaps as other young men are. But he is evidently every inch a soldier, and one who, with utter disregard of his own life, never neglected a precaution, or showed himself indifferent to the advantages of science. If any explanation be asked of how and why General Gordon was able to lead a Chinese army to almost constant victory six years later, I believe the key is furnished in these letters, by his attention to detail and devotion to duty in the Crimea, on the Danube, and in Armenia. This side of the character of the man

who has held Khartoum during all these months
of silence and isolation should be brought into
prominence. His countrymen must well know that
he at least will stand to his post to the last, and
we believe that when he sends the first ray of light,
and it will come from him, out of his prison-house,
it will show that he has held his own, and more
than held it, while everywhere else there have
been confusion, retreat, and recrimination, with
loss of character and the sowing of a plentiful
crop of evils for the future in lands where the
power of Englishmen will not enable them to
stay save by the exhibition of the same attributes
which planted their ancestors in them in the past.

It is well that at this moment we should be
as strongly reminded as possible of that practical
side of General Gordon's character which has
made him the successful leader of armies and the
vigorous administrator of vast provinces; and this
record of his early career before he had done
anything more famous than that which he is
doing now, his duty to his country in face of the
enemy, may be acceptable both to his admirers
and to that large mass of Englishmen who, without

care for the intricacies of a political question, see an almost solitary * Englishman surrounded by a wide and ever-widening sea of rebellion and fanaticism, having little or no promise of effectual help, save what he may derive from his faith in his countrymen, and pronounce his abandonment, without fear of persons or of names, a shameful betrayal of a too-confiding officer, and an enduring stigma on the national honour.

"But one sad losel soils a name for aye."

DEMETRIUS C. BOULGER.

June 24, 1884.

* No disparagement is intended, because their names are not mentioned, of either Colonel Donald Stewart or the other Englishman, Mr. Power, now in Khartoum. All who know the former will feel sure that in him General Gordon has found an attached and energetic lieutenant.

PART I.

GENERAL GORDON'S LETTERS

FROM THE CRIMEA, ETC.

—◦—

Pembroke Dock, Aug. 18, 1854.—I hope you and
all the family are quite well, and like Gibraltar.*
It must be very warm now with you. The harvest
here is just beginning; it is a very good one, and
the weather, as yet, has been very favourable. This
county is a great corn county, very little green
crops being grown. We had another launch on
Thursday of a twenty-six gun screw steamer. I
have seen five launches since I have been here.
The Queen's yacht is now getting on fast. She will
go twenty miles per hour when finished, and is
of immense length. I have been very busy in

---

* At this time General Gordon's father, the late Lieut.-General
H. W. Gordon, of the Royal Artillery, was stationed at Gibraltar.

B

doing plans for another fort, to be built at the
entrance of the haven.   I pity the officers and
men who will have to live in these forts, as they
are in the most desolate places, seven miles from
any town, and fifteen from any conveyance.   If
they garrison them with artillery, it will require
for Pembroke Dock and defences more than a
battalion, which will necessitate an equal augmen-
tation of that force.

Pembroke Dock, Oct. 5, 1854.— —— says there
were no artillery engaged in the battle of Alma; so
that —— was safe out of that.   I hope you get
the newspapers regularly. . . .   The change of dress
is a great nuisance, as my coat is almost new,
and I am afraid it will not alter into a tunic.
We are to keep our frock-coat, which is to be
open in front, with a red waistcoat; our gold-lace
trousers are to be dispensed with, but the cocked
hat is to be retained.   There is a very amusing
bit in the paper about Sir G. Brown having been
nearly taken by the Cossacks; mind and read
it. . . . You ought to get every newspaper that is
published, as I send every one I get.   Do you take
Jackson's Journal? if not, I can send you that also
if you like.

Pembroke Dock, Nov. 30, 1854.—You will not be surprised at hearing that I got my orders for Corfu yesterday, as I suspect you used your interest to have me sent there instead of to the Crimea. It is a great shame of you. However, I must not grumble, as I am lucky in not being sent to the West Indies, or New Zealand. I see my father's promotion in the *Times,* which I am sorry for, as it will leave him idle. How does he like the prospect of coming home, and when do you think it will take place? I have no idea when I go from here, but if I had my wish I would remain for two months more, as I am comfortably settled. If I cannot remain here as employed, I shall ask for two months' leave and stay here. It is a great inconvenience in our corps, that of being ordered away at a minute's notice. I really do like this place, now I have got used to it. I have a great deal of time to myself, and have some very nice companions. Captain —— has returned with his wife, a very stylish person (an ardent admirer of Mr. Molyneux*). I like her very much. If you do come home, I dare say I shall see you before I go. I do not know what to do with my horse. I have a great mind to take it out, if I could for

* The late Rev. Capel Molyneux.

nothing. We hear a great deal about raising two extra batteries of artillery, but nothing of any increase to ourselves.

Portsmouth, Dec. 12, 1854.—I will write now that I have a little leisure, and tell you that I leave for the Crimea on Friday, *viâ* Marseilles. I go out in charge of the huts, and I think it is a very good thing. I have got a quantity of warm clothing, and, through the kindness of the Agent Cox, I have made a very complete outfit. I will write to you when I start. I only got my order at Pembroke on the 4th. I left Pembroke the same day and went to the War Office; saw Colonel Matson, who told me to go at once to Portsmouth. I did so, and arrived there on the 6th. I have been employed ever since, from morn to night, putting the huts on board. I was at first to go out in one of the colliers; but Sir F. Smith, who is very kind, got me off. I am now to go *viâ* Marseilles. I will write you an account of the journey later on. . . . I am extremely lucky in going by Marseilles, as I am such a bad sailor. . . . Each of the huts holds twenty-four men, or two captains and four subalterns, or two field officers, or one general. They are rather pretty in appearance. What a strong place Portsmouth seems! . . . I have taken out a good supply of tea, because I knew you would scold me if I did not.

Marseilles, Dec. 16, 1854.—I suppose you have heard before this that I am travelling overland? although, had I known that they did not prepay our passage, I should have thought twice about it. . . . I think it is very hard not to give us anything before starting. . . . I intend writing to you and —— once every mail. I left London by half-past eight o'clock on the 14th, got to Paris at five o'clock p.m. on the 15th, left the same evening at eight o'clock, and entered Lyons at six o'clock the next morning. From Lyons I went down the Rhone to Valence, and from Valence to Marseilles by rail, reaching the latter place at seven o'clock very tired. The country from Calais to Paris was very flat and dull, and that between Paris and Lyons I did not see, as it was dark. Lyons is a beautiful city, with very fine bridges; there are 45,000 Frenchmen * in it. The voyage down the Rhone was also splendid—such pretty towns and villages, and vineyards and rivers; the mountains in the

* General Gordon evidently meant able-bodied men. The population of Lyons and its suburbs in 1876 was 342,815.

distance are capped with snow. I luckily met
my commanding officer at the railway terminus
at Paris, and we are now together. We are going
out, I think I told you, to superintend the putting
up of the huts. We leave this (D.V.) on Monday,
at three p.m., and touch at Messina. It takes
six and a half days to get to Constantinople, and
they charge £17 for the passage. . . . Twenty
French doctors go out in the same vessel; it is
called the *Thabor*. Several officers arrived from
the Crimea last night; they say that —— was
working very hard and doing capitally. Among
them is Sir De Lacy Evans.

Hôtel de l'Angleterre, Constantinople, Dec. 26, 1854.
—We arrived here in safety at three o'clock, and I
shall take up my tale from Marseilles. We had a
rough time of it the first night, and the poor French
soldiers, of whom there were 320 on board, without
any shelter, must have suffered considerably from
cold; they had no covering, and in spite of the wet,
cold, and bad weather, they kept up their health,
however, and their high spirits also, when our men
would have mutinied. We passed the Straits of
Bonifacio, and arrived at Messina on the 22nd.
I landed and saw the town, which has suffered

immensely from the cholera, losing 22,000 people out of a population of 66,000. My father must recollect the town, which is near Scylla. The straits are not more than one and a half miles broad. We left the same night, and passing through Cerigo and the mainland, reached the Piræus, and went on shore there. Piræus is five miles from Athens, and 800 of the 3rd Buffs are stationed there at this time. It is a miserable place. We drove to the Acropolis, which is a beautiful ruin, and the view is very fine from the top. The town of Athens is very ugly and dirty, and the country looks uncommonly barren. We left the same day, and passed through the Archipelago, reaching the Dardanelles at one o'clock on Christmas Day. They did not seem to me to be very strongly fortified, as the forts, though numerous, are open at the rear, and overlooked by the heights behind. The English consul has built a splendid palace at the Castle of Asia. We stopped at Gallipoli, but none of our troops are there now, and we left the same night for Constantinople, which is twelve hours' passage from the former place. The passage was rough in the Sea of Marmora. We arrived at Constantinople at three o'clock, and I must say I was rather disappointed with the view. The city is much lower than I expected, and the finest buildings I saw were the hospital at Scutari, the Seraglio, and the Russian Embassy. Of course, you know all about the state of the town when one lands, and of the filth, bad drainage, etc., of the streets. The Duke of Cambridge is at the palace; he is in rather better health now, and, I believe, will go home in the *Ripon* to-morrow. The *Royal Albert* has wrung its rudder, and is lying disabled at Balaclava. Admiral Dundas goes home to-morrow in the *Britannia*. Sir Edmund Lyons succeeds him. . . . We passed a transport on fire (having, I am sorry to say, warm clothing on board) close to Scutari. Four of our hut vessels have passed through, so we shall have to leave this immediately. I told —— to mention to the Duke who I was, and that I had asked after him. There was a serious fracas to-day between the police and the French troops, in which three of the latter were seriously wounded. I went over to-day (Dec. 27) to Scutari, where our wounded are; they have now everything they want, and all comforts. Major Staveley left for England on November 24, and young Staveley went on to the Crimea to-day. We do not leave this until the morning. There are accounts of numerous sorties on our lines by the Russians, but of course I cannot form any idea about their importance at present. We have given up Eupatoria to the Turks, who are 40,000 strong, under Omar Pasha, and all in excellent order. Our new guns and mortars are expected to be ready to open in a fortnight. Who do you think we met at the *table d'hôte,* but —— ? I spoke to him, and he desired to be remembered to all of you ; he has been out here, he told me, for four months with Admiral Dundas, and leaves to-morrow. I shall write to you from Balaclava, and tell you all the news I can collect.

Balaclava, Jan. 3, 1855.—I arrived at the above place, where I am now living, on January 1. I came up in the *Golden Fleece* with the 39th, and took charge of ——'s box and letters, which you gave into the care of Colonel Munro. Captain Hudson was very kind. They gave me the latest news from Gibraltar, and I was very glad to hear you are all well. I went up to Sir J. Burgoyne the day I arrived and reported myself; he was very civil. Enderby * I also visited ; he looks very well, and in very good health. He has a very substantial hut, and is, you will like to know, quite comfortable.

* General Gordon's brother, the late Major-General Enderby Gordon, R.A. Where the name of Henry occurs, it refers to his other brother, Sir Henry Gordon.

The roads are bad beyond description, being quite a morass the whole way up. I have not yet seen Sebastopol, and do not hear anything about the siege. We hear a gun now and then, but they are generally fired by the Russians at the French. No one seems to interest himself about the siege, but all appear to be engaged in foraging expeditions for grub, etc. I hope to tell you something of what is going on in my next letter, but at present we are at a standstill. We are, however, getting up large guns and immense supplies of ammunition, and I believe the French are also advancing in their works. We have ample rations served out to us, and there is no want of anything now in that line. I have not yet got my luggage, but expect it daily in the *Alster* screw collier. About 300 huts are here, but the transport is a great difficulty in the way of their being put up at the front. However, the engineer says that the railroad will be ready in six weeks or less. The weather continues very mild, with rain and a few showers of snow. I saw Mr. Russell, the *Times* correspondent, last night; they have given him a house here. I have just seen Enderby, who tells me that Major Swinton was found dead in his bed this morning, from either apoplexy or charcoal.

Balaclava, Jan. 8, 1855.—Very many thanks for your kind letter of November 27, which I received to-day from England, and am delighted to hear that you are all well. Your anxiety about Enderby, so far as we short-sighted creatures can see, will be relieved, I hope, when I tell you that he is in a capital hut, and looks much better than I ever saw him; he says his health has never been better, and of course he is well fed. I have got a splendid outfit, and two chamois-leather vests and drawers. I am very glad that I shall not require any assistance from my father, as I am now going to hand him enough to cover all my expenses. I am sorry to say that Lieutenant Daunt, 9th Regiment, and another officer of some 60th Regiment, were frozen to death last night; and that Lieutenant Ramsbottom, of the 97th, and two officers of the 93rd Regiment were smothered with charcoal. So I shall keep a sharp look-out not to use it. We have about a foot of snow on the ground, and a sharp frost, which is a great advantage, as it hardens the roads, and is much better for the men than the wet weather. Omar Pasha landed here to attend a council of war yesterday. The troops he has with him are at present very sickly. The railway is being laid down. We have only put up two huts as yet, but hope to do better soon. I have met a great many friends here. I am living, as I told you before, in a house in Balaclava, which is very comfortable, and always get plenty to eat. The streets of this village are quite a sight, what with six or seven hundred Zouaves carrying shell to our batteries, Turks mending roads and other drudgery, the swell English cavalry and horse artillery carrying rations, officers in every conceivable costume foraging for eatables, etc. The mud was too dreadful, but it is now frozen, and the walking is pretty good. The camels look very miserable. Nothing is going on at head-quarters. Do not think I have not got a good outfit. Even Enderby admires my coat! Do not send me anything, but send them to Enderby. ——, between you and me, has not been properly taken care of, but I hope he will get some warm things here. Do not say anything about it.

Balaclava, Jan. 18, 1855.—I ought to have written last mail, but did not write, luckily enough, as the letters never went after all. We are still at a standstill out here, but hope to make some stir soon, as the batteries will open in about a fortnight. Through the smallness of our numbers, we have given up the Inkerman batteries to the French, who will for the future victual a division from this place, which will add to the confusion, and that is now pretty considerable. General Canrobert moves about in great state; he always has a great banner with him and an escort of Spahis. Their Zouaves carry up a great quantity of shot and shell for us. We are commencing to arm our batteries. Captain —— has been very kind. Mind and mention to his wife that I have told you, as it is unusual for a brigade major to be civil to a strange subaltern. Our huts are not yet put up in any great number, but they are progressing rapidly. Bread is very dear here; we pay as much as two shillings for a small loaf. Most extraordinary prices are paid for some things, as you have seen. As I am in a house, I have lent Enderby my stove, which is a very good one. His hut is a very comfortable one. I slept up there one night. This work certainly suits him. I am rather surprised at our getting another half battalion, after the whole one given this time last year. It will put me up twenty-six places. There is not much doing here at present. The Russians and French keep up a little fire, but our trenches are silent. I saw Sebastopol yesterday for the first time, and do not think I ever saw a prettier city; it looks quite open, and a Russian steamer was cruising about inside the harbour. Two of their steamers came out the other day and bombarded the French lines for two hours, but our vessels were unable to move out to attack them, as their steam was not up. For the future it will be always up. The surrounding country is a beautiful one, and very picturesque.

Camp, before Sebastopol, Feb. 2, 1855.—As far as comfort is concerned, I assure you, my dear ——, I could not be more comfortable in England, as I have a double tent, and have dug out the bottom of it, so that it is quite warm. . . . We are doing nothing here, and I hope you will not believe all the atrocious fibs which are told in the papers of our misery. The French are pushing on close to the Flagstaff Battery; they have now 100,000 men out here. . . . I am making lots of sketches, and will send some home soon. . . . The Arch-Dukes, who have recovered from their defeat, have again appeared, and had a reconnaissance of our positions the other day at Inkerman. The health of the men has improved greatly; the wet is what makes them ill. The weather is now very mild by day, quite hot some days, and a little frosty at night;

but, on the whole, we could not have better weather in England.

Camp, Feb. 12, 1855.—Nothing much is doing, except repairing our batteries and getting ready for our second siege. The French * have taken our Inkerman attack, so that our army is in the middle, and for the moment in rather a secondary position. . . . There are really no hardships for the officers; the men are the sufferers, and that is partly their own fault, as they are like children, thinking everything is to be done for them. The French soldier looks out for himself, and consequently fares much better.

Camp, before Sebastopol, Feb. 17, 1855.—As to the letter of the 15th being so short, if you knew what a deal I had to do, and what little opportunity I have to get any news, you would not wonder at its brevity. Now I have finished with your letter. The sketch of the right attack I have not yet got, but will send it next time. The night of February 14th I was on duty in the trenches, and if you look at the plan I sent you

* They had just taken over the positions on Mount Inkerman and Victoria Ridge. See Kinglake's History, vol. vi.

and the small sketch enclosed, I will explain what
I had to do. The French that night determined
to join their sentries on their right and our sentries
on our left in advance of their and our trenches,
so as to prevent the Russians coming up the ravine
and then turning against our flank. They determined to make a lodgment in the ruined house B,
and to run a trench up the hill to the left of
this, while I was told to make a communication
by rifle-pits from the caves C to the ruined
house B.

I got, after some trouble, eight men with picks
and shovels, and asked the captain of the advance
trench, Captain ——, of the 4th, to give me five
double sentries to throw out in advance. It was
the first time he had been on duty here ; and, as for
myself, I never had, although I kept that to myself.
I led forward the sentries, going at the head of the
party, and found the sentries of the advance had
not held the caves, which they ought to have done
after dark, so there was just a chance of the Russians
being in them. I went on, however, and, though
I did not like it, explored the caves almost alone.
We then left two sentries on the hill above the
caves, and went back to get round and post two
sentries below the caves. However, just as soon

as we showed ourselves outside the caves and below them, bang! bang! went two rifles, the bullets hitting the ground close to us. The sentries with me retired in a rare state of mind, and my working party bolted, and were stopped with great difficulty. What had really happened was this. It was not a Russian attack, but the two sentries whom I had placed above the caves *had fired at us,* lost their caps, and bolted to the trench. Nothing after this would induce the sentries to go out, so I got the working party to go forward with me. The Russians had, on the report of our shots, sent us a shower of bullets, their picket not being more than 150 yards away. I set the men to work, and then went down to the bottom of the ravine, and found the French in strength hard at work also. Having told them who we were, I returned to the trench, where I met Colonel ——, of the 1st Royals. I warned him, if he went out, he would be sure to be hit by his own sentries or the Russians. He would go, however, and a moment afterwards was hit in the breast, the ball going through his coats, slightly grazing his ribs, and passing out again without hurting him. I stayed with my working party all night, and got home very tired.

C

I should have told you that when going out myself in the first instance to find the trench and caves, I passed our advance sentries and went down to D, about 180 yards from our lines, and very nearly walked into the town by mistake. The French have thrown up a battery for us, under our engineers, in the advance of the right attack. It mounts twelve guns to fire on the tower, and they are also very hard at work at Inkerman. Bosquet's division is said to be going to meet Liprandi; but no one knows for certain. Our batteries have arrived, but not enough ammunition has come yet. Jones * has taken the command of us, and has been over all our works. Our army is a mere handful, and we are told now to wait for more artillery. I have no notion when we begin. Our attack can advance no further, for the hill drops too rapidly. I wish they had not given the medal, as we have not yet got the place. The line officers are too much disposed to stay in the little huts and holes in the parallel when the men are working for us, and leave them to do more as they like than they should. We have capital rations, and all the men have warm clothing, and more than enough of that.

* The late Sir Harry Jones.

They, of course, grumble and growl a good deal. The contrast with the French in this respect is not to our advantage. The railway progresses slowly. Some buffaloes have arrived. The news here is very scanty, and the lies very plentiful; this, for instance—we heard that Omar Pasha had beaten the Russians back from the north side, which is all a crammer. I really have just now too much to do for extensive correspondence, what with plans, trench work, and hutting, which I still look after. All of Biddulph's drawings are very good, but the others, generally speaking, are bad. I can think of no other news that I can tell you. The Russians are very quiet indeed now, which, I should think, is on account of their ammunition. You would stare to see how they have strewn the ground with shot and shell.

Camp, before Sebastopol, Feb. 21, 1855.—I suppose by this time you are in England. We are still in winter, but it now seems about breaking up, as young grass and crocuses are appearing. . . . The Russians made a small sortie last night, but our men were on the look-out, and they retreated. Five Russian deserters came in on the night of the 20th; they say the Dukes are with them, that they have lots of money and drink, and that numbers of Poles would desert if they could. The Turks have thrashed the Russians at Eupatoria, although they brought 100 guns against them. I still live with Major ——, whom I like very much. You will excuse my bad writing, as my ink is frozen, and getting a dip breaks the nib of my pen. I can form no opinion when we shall open fire. The railway will be complete in three weeks, and I do not think it will be until after that. There is a report rife here that General ——, of the French, has been discovered giving information to the Russians, and that papers proving his treason have been found in his tent. A Pole brought the information from the town. This general is, they say, a prisoner at Kherson. . . . The Russians gave the French a little surprise last night. The latter have been making a battery of fifteen guns at Inkerman, for the attack on the Malakoff tower (which the Russians are now pulling down), when, to their astonishment, the Russians threw up in one night a battery of twenty guns immediately opposite. The Turks beat the Russians off at Eupatoria, with a loss of 150 men killed; they themselves lost 97, and 277 wounded. I am quite well, and like the work very much.

Camp, before Sebastopol, Feb. 28, 1855.—The
French attacked a battery which the Russians, as
I told you, had made on the open ground, 600 yards
from their works, near the Malakoff tower. They
attacked in three columns, but found the Russians
well prepared. The Zouaves carried the battery;
but the Russian reserve coming up, they were
driven back—their own reserves, a battalion of
marines, declining to come to the scratch.

The French suffered greatly, and own to 200 killed.
One thing is positive—the battery must be taken,
as it will never do to let the Russians make
batteries where they like, at that distance in
advance of their works. The French Imperial
Guard went over that way to-day, so that I think
they are going to try it again; if they will not do
it, we must. The Russians had an hour's armistice yesterday to bury the dead of the above
conflict; and all round our trenches the Russians
came out of their rifle-pits—which are marked in
the sketch—and called out for tobacco. They have
fifty of these in the top and twenty in the lower
part of their lines. A shot from one of the latter
as nearly as possible did for me; the bullet was
fired not 180 yards off, and passed an inch above
my nut into a bank I was passing. They are very

good marksmen. Their bullet is large and pointed.
—— dined with us last night; he is very well, and
seems to like it. ——, a captain of his regiment,
is very kind to him. I do not think he wants
anything now.

March 2, 1855.—We are going to make a new
battery for five guns in the advance trench, to the
left of the place where the zigzag enters the
parallel. It will be commenced to-night. The
Russians have made another battery, 300 yards *in
advance* of the one the French attacked. This looks
serious,* as they will be able to make an entrenched
camp behind it. Liprandi's army was seen marching
over the heights to this point. I hope the French
will take it. Jones is a great addition; he under-
stands his work. I think it will not be long before
we begin, as most of the ammunition is up. We
hear that Sir J. B—— is recalled; and that General
Simpson is to be chief of the staff; that Generals
Airey and Estcourt are offered brigades, or else to

* In another letter General Gordon writes on the same subject
under date—

"*Camp, before Sebastopol, March* 2, 1855.—This is rather too cool,
and I am sorry to say that the French do not seem inclined to try
and take it, after their failure the other night; it must be done, however, if not by them, then by us, as the Russians will be able to
make an entrenched camp for 12,000 or 14,000 men behind these
works."

go home—which it will be I do not know. The huts are being erected pretty rapidly, and 1500 Croats have come here for carrying purposes. We ought to number 24,000 men by this time. I have got my allowance for horses, which I shall send home as soon as I can get a Treasury bill for the amount. The Russians sent a shell into our parties who were cutting wood, or rather digging roots, near the camp. This is almost three miles. The French also have been firing rockets at a tremendous range into the arsenal, nearly two and a half miles. These rockets are made with a very short stick, and fired with very little elevation.

Camp, before Sebastopol, March 10, 1855.—We are doing very little just now, but I think we shall commence our second bombardment in a very short time. The French are very close to the town in one part, not more than eighty yards. They have run a mine under the flagstaff battery, and have also a very large battery of mortars opposite to it. The Russians cannot show their heads above the works. The former have a wire stretched from picket to picket, three feet below the top of their parapet, so that the Russians trip up when they run over the parapet, and get bayoneted by the French below. They are splendid soldiers, and capital shots with their rifles. We have made a new battery for six guns in our advanced work. The men are looking very well, and the weather is beautiful. Thermometer 84° to-day. I do not think I was ever in better health, and enjoy the work amazingly. It is very odd that the Russians never fire on us (the English), unless we begin it. The place looks very strong. We heard of the death of the Czar the other day, and sent in word to Menschikoff. The French now muster 80,000, and we 23,000; but we are deficient in artillery. Colonel —— is very kind. I went and dined with him a few days ago. I have a great many inquiries after you from every one who knew you at Gibraltar. I hope that you all keep your health, and that you had a good passage home. Many thanks for the good things you have sent me; but we can now get almost anything at Balaclava. I went with —— to see Enderby to-day. He was out; but I met him afterwards. He is very well. The Russians have thrown up a new large work in advance of the tower of Malakoff. They do not believe the death of the Czar. We shall open fire again shortly, and I hope this will soon put an end to this protracted seige. My expenses out here are very small indeed, not more than £8 per month. I have had many inquiries after my father, who seems to have been greatly liked in Gibraltar. There was an interesting incident last Thursday. A Russian steamer was lying snugly up at the east end of the harbour, thinking she was quite safe. Our artillery got up a surprise, and at break of day opened on her, and struck her six times, disabling her, and making the crew leave her. George —— is getting very fat, and looks so very well. General Jones does a great deal of good, and is very much looked up to by every one. Three thousand of the French Imperial Guard are here— very fine-looking men. They are not sent into the trenches. Weather beautiful; very much like England in the spring. Crocuses cover the ground.

Camp, before Sebastopol, March 17, 1855.—The Russians have just heard of the Emperor's death,* and tolled the bells for him. They asked for a truce for three days, and on being refused, threw up a work right in front of their position on the Mamelon

* The Emperor Nicholas died early on the morning of the 3rd of March, 1855. On his death-bed, strangely enough, he received despatches from the Crimea, which he handed over, as no longer concerning him, to his son and successor, the late Czar Alexander II.

Hill, which will annoy us rather. They are very brave. I am going to send home a plan when I get time, but we are rather hard worked at present. . . . We lost one of our captains, named Craigie, by a splinter of a shell in the ravine near the picket house. I am glad to say he was a serious man. The shell burst above him, and, by what is called chance, struck him in the back, killing him at once. The French and the Russians have frequent scrimmages; but they do not get on very well with us. Very ludicrous things occur occasionally. For instance, on a shell falling near a working party, twenty of them fired at the shell, and the other lot fired in mistake at them; the wind up being, two men wounded. The Russians sneak out at dusk and, when our men are being relieved, steal our gabions—regular thieving. However, we caught one last night. —— is so fat, and looks so well! He is a very happy man.

Camp, before Sebastopol, March 23, 1855.—The French are very cautious with the Russians, who hold rifle-pits within thirty yards of their trenches, and from which the French cannot dislodge them. This affects our advance, as unless the French also moved forward, we should be left with our flanks uncovered. General Jones, R.E., is a great acquisition. He is about the trenches at daybreak. Sir John Burgoyne has departed for England, after leaving a very complimentary order about our exertions. No volunteering for me, as I have nothing to gain! The Russians are said to be short of ammunition, which seems likely, as they do not fire very much. Our artillery does great damage to a new work they have just erected on the Mamelon; the practice is capital. The railway is progressing rapidly. It is not very far from this spot. I could not be more comfortable than I am. I have everything I want. We are very well off, and the men look first-rate. Two Polish engineer officers came in as deserters the other day, and gave very valuable information about the enemy's works. The country near Sebastopol is so like the Downs, and the climate also is so similar, that we can scarcely believe that we are in Russia. There are quantities of bulbous roots about just coming into bloom—hyacinths, etc. There are wolves and deer in the plain of the Tchernaya. Despite home reports to the contrary, no Russian has crossed the river near us for four months. If people here knew what trash appears in the papers, they would stare. Every one out here is sick and

tired of the bygone grievances. Nothing is easier
than to find fault. Biddulph's sketches are very
truthful, and give a very good idea of the
country. I have got a relic of Inkerman for my
father—the brass off a Russian musket. There
are a few Russian forage caps lying about; but
very little is now to be seen of where this great
battle was fought. Biddulph's sketch of this combat
is very good. We are ready to open fire and to
push on our batteries, but cannot until the French
take the Mamelon Hill, which, with their army
of 110,000, they ought to do.

Camp, before Sebastopol, March 31, 1855.—I know
you will be in a bother if I do not write this mail,
so that, although I am in a great hurry, I will send
a line. The field officer, Colonel Kelly, 34th Regiment, is not dead, but taken prisoner. We heard
from Captain Montague, who is very well treated,
and is in Osten Lacken's house. We had an armistice
for two hours, to bury the dead of the sortie last
Saturday. —— came down and looked about
him. The Russian officers came up and talked to
us; they do not look particularly clean. We are
not doing very much at present, but hope to do
something soon.

Camp, before Sebastopol, April 7, 1855.—We are still here in our old position ; although our works are advancing considerably, and everything is now ready for our commencing again. Since the sortie nothing of importance has occurred, except the throwing up of new batteries on both sides. I am sorry to say poor Bainbridge was killed by a shell on April 4 ; he was in the Royal Engineers, and a son of the general. Lord Raglan is going to put up a tablet at his own expense. Twenty-five thousand Turks are coming here from Eupatoria, and 5000 of them arrived to-day. Our army now numbers 28,000 ; and the French 110,000. The Russians certainly are inferior to none ; their work is stupendous. Imagine our trenches presenting a front to them of upwards of twenty miles ! We turned them out of one of their rifle-pits the other day, by making a rifle-screen above them, which looked into theirs, and enabled us to enfilade them. Their shell practice is beautiful, but it would surprise you if you saw how perfectly harmless shells generally are. Tell my father that at 750 yards they sent a shot from a 30-pounder through twenty feet of earth ; eighteen feet is generally thought to be shot-proof. Also tell him that Alderson's platforms do not answer for mortars at all. They send, however, 13″ shells upwards of two miles. We imagine that Lord Raglan has delayed our commencing until peace or war is decided at Vienna, and that we shall know next mail. More than 500 rounds per gun are up in the batteries. The railway progresses rapidly; there are no locomotive engines on it, but stationary ones on the top of the hills. The Russians have made their new work on the Mamelon very strong, but our shells are doing a great deal of damage to it. The fresh battery of artillery has not arrived yet, but is expected daily. ——'s brother is with it; he will be senior ordnance surgeon here. The men are looking very healthy and well. They are very comfortably off in their huts ; but you get so used to a tent that you do not feel it at all ; your whole possessions are around you, and everything can be got out in a minute. Besides, if you get cold you can go to bed without any bother about parades, etc. I am afraid I am becoming field-officer-like ; all my things are getting too small. I must write to ——, but I cannot just yet, as I am busy finishing a plan which I want to copy for my father.

Camp, before Sebastopol, April 13, 1855.— We re-opened fire last Monday, the 9th instant, and took our friends the Russians by surprise. The fire still continues, and the enemy's works are very much injured. Our losses in officers are Lieutenants Twyford and Douglas, R.N., Luce, R.A., and Sinclair, R.A., killed; Captain Crofton, R.E., severely wounded; and in the four days since we opened fire thirty men killed and the same number wounded, which is slight in comparison with the loss the enemy must have sustained. The weather, which was bad on Monday and Tuesday, has since very much improved. The Russian fire, although good, is not nearly so brisk as it used to be, which may be on account of shortness of ammunition, or from want of gunners, their old ones being dead. Our batteries are a little knocked about, but there are not more than two guns disabled by the enemy's shot. One Lancaster gun and a 13″ mortar burst on our side; no one was hurt, I am glad to say. Omar Pasha is here, and has sent 10,000 Turks from his army to assist us. The French keep up their fire very well, and have reduced that of the Russians very much. Our 13″ mortars do a great deal of harm to the Russians. The Russians have dropped three 13″ mortar shells on our powder magazines, which have stood intact, and that speaks very well for them. George Bent has the direction of this attack, while Major Gordon is ill from his wounds. The electric

wire was cut by a shell the day before yesterday, in
the Woronzoff road. General Jones rides about, and
is the most active man on the spot. I am extremely comfortable, and could wish for nothing
better than I have at present. The other night,
when we were arming No. 7 battery, the French
were firing rockets, one of which struck short and
remained just in front of the party who were
pulling the guns, lighting us up finely. The
Russians twigged us, and fired a few rounds, but
they didn't know that we were busy placing our
guns. One of the guns was struck in the muzzle
and disabled, but no men were hurt. The artillery
practice on our side is remarkably good, but our
fuzes are infamous. You must forgive this *official*
letter as I have no news. The men are healthy and
well fed.

Camp, before Sebastopol, April 20, 1855.—I take
up my story from the 13th April. On the 14th,
Lieutenant Michell, R.A., was killed in the right
attack. On the 15th, Captain Crofton, R.E., who
was wounded on the 12th, died from the effects of
his wounds. The French the same night blew up
six small mines, thus making a small trench in front
of the flagstaff battery. The Russians ran forward

the moment of explosion and tried to occupy the
trench, but the French drove them back, and by
pulling out the tamping of the mine made a sub-
terranean communication to the trench. I cannot
say much for the enterprise of our allies. They
are afraid to do anything, and, consequently, quite
cramp our movements, as you will easily understand that if one part of the trenches is pushed
on before the other parts, the advanced sections
will be liable to be attacked and outflanked by
the Russians. I think we might have assaulted on
the Monday, but the French do not seem to care
about it. The garrison is 25,000 men, and we heard
afterwards that on that day only 800 men were
in the place, as the rest had gone to repel an attack
(fancied) of ours at Inkerman. General Bizot,
of the French Engineers, was killed to-day (15th)
by a rifle bullet. Green, an assistant Engineer,
was also wounded by a bullet on the 16th. A
13″ shell fell on one of our powder magazines and
blew it up, killing one man and wounding six.
This is the first we have had blown up, while the
Russians have had four. There are frequent fires
in the town from the shells. I went to Bizot's
funeral, as General Jones wished it, and saw
Omar Pasha and Canrobert there. Canrobert is a

D

mountebank, a horrid little fellow. Our fire slackened on the 18th, why we do not know. On the 18th, King, R.E., was hit in the hip by a bullet, but not seriously. The Russians keep up a constant fire on the head of our sap every night. 19th, I went with Enderby to the reconnaissance made by Omar Pasha and the Turks. The latter look very fine troops, and work well. We drove the Russians back seven miles, and enjoyed the country very much after being camped so long. The Russians were about 2000 strong. The country is beautiful.

Camp, April 20, 1855.—I write to tell you that last night we took some rifle-pits in front of the Redan after a sharp fight, in which Captain Owen, R.E., and Lieutenant Baynes, R.E., were dangerously wounded; Colonel Edgington and Captain Lemprière, 77th Regiment, killed; and Lieutenant Trevor, 55th Regiment, wounded; 70 men killed and wounded. We do not know the Russian loss, but it must be considerable. There is no news but this. Lord Stratford de Redcliffe has come up, I believe for change of air. Owen was struck through the thigh, and has since lost his leg; Baynes was hit in the chest and arm.

Camp, April 30, 1855.—We are still in the same position as when I last wrote, having almost ceased firing from our batteries, and the Russians doing ditto. Poor King died last Sunday week. He was thought to be out of danger, but got fever and died the same day. Owen and Baynes are getting on very well, although the former has lost his leg. Nothing of any consequence has occurred since my last letter. The French had a sortie made upon them on the 25th, and fought for three hours. There has been a grand review of the French army by Canrobert, who is not very popular at present on account of his not pushing on the siege. Omar Pasha has set out with 15,000 Turks for Eupatoria, leaving 10,000 here. The Sardinians do not come up to the mark. The communication by electric telegraph is complete. We can hear from London in twelve hours, and it is to be thrown open to officers, at £1 12s. 6d. per message. We are pushing our batteries forward as fast as possible, but cannot advance our trenches until the French take the Mamelon, as it would enfilade our advanced works. We are very comfortable as far as grub, etc., is concerned; but want to see some result in our work, as the summer is very near, and we ought to be doing something. I do not think the Russians can do us any harm; but unless we take the place we can do them as little. . . . I must conclude this very stupid letter (which is not my fault, as none of the three nations—French, English, or Russians—will do anything).

Camp, May 4, 1855.—Many thanks for your kind letter and for the Indian ink. The weather here is beautiful, not too hot at present. On the evening of May 1st the French attacked and carried a small counterguard in front of the flagstaff battery, taking eight or ten Cohorn mortars. The fight lasted four hours; they are now forty yards from the works. I went over to head-quarters to see Enderby, who is quite well. On the night of the 2nd, Lieutenant Carter, R.E., and Lieutenant Curtis, 46th Regiment, were killed in our attack by grape shot. I went down to Balaclava yesterday and saw ——. He is very well and very busy. An expedition of 2500 British and 7500 French is going to Kertch, or some place near it. Sir G. Brown commands; they start to-day. I believe the object is to stop the supplies which come by that place from Asia. There is nothing going on, that I am aware of. The Turks, to the number of 7500, made a reconnaissance yesterday, and drove the

Cossacks back from the plains of Balaclava. I took advantage of it to ride over the redoubts which the Turks lost during the battle of Balaclava. I am sure they were little to blame for it, as you can ride over any part of the ditches. A few skeleton horses lie about, one saddled and with the bit in his mouth just as he fell. Nothing else would show that there had been an action fought there. The plain is covered with wild thyme, which when marched upon by the troops gives out a delicious smell. It is a beautiful country, and a great change from the bare ground and rocky soil of our encampment. We are very well off as far as supplies are concerned, but we are still waiting for the French. I hope when this siege is over we shall (if the war goes on) separate our armies. Do not fret yourself about volunteering. I shall not volunteer. Poor Carter! I had known him for years; he is to be buried to-day. We have a great deal to regret in the way of good working clergymen. You will see by the newspapers that we have again stopped firing in a very mysterious way, which is said to be owing to the French, as we could have gone on. They have continued to bully us into firing, saying that they would take the Kamschatka lunette after the third day's fire, which,

however, they did not do. Captain Owen is going
on as well as possible, and will leave for England
very soon.

Camp, May 20, 1855.—On the evening of the
11th the Russians made a sortie on our trenches;
it was pouring in torrents at the time, and blowing
hard. They came up, and ten of them entered the
advance battery. These were killed. One of them
was seen feeling along the guns to spike them. The
guns had been previously temporarily spiked by the
artillery. The Russians fought very well, and lost
a good many men, some of whom they carried off.
They left, however, eight or ten dead in our
trenches, one of whom was an officer, and two were
buglers. One of the latter was shot as he was
blowing the advance on the top of the trench.
We lost Captain Edwards and five men of the 68th
Regiment killed and nineteen wounded. The only
prisoner taken declared that they had been pro-
mised not to be taken against the English, but
against the French, and that they were deceived
by their officers. On the 16th Lord Raglan and the
Sardinian general visited the trenches. Nothing
else has occurred since I wrote. Councils of war
are continually held. We have now 700 rounds per

gun in the batteries, and before we only had 500.
We shall open fire also with many more guns, and I
do not doubt of our taking the place, as, by their
own despatches, they suffered immensely last time ;
and now, in addition to all our old batteries, we
have many new ones, and all of these much
nearer. I hope we shall not have to make
peace on bad terms, as our position is not at
all desperate. I wish the emperor would recall
Canrobert. The French are disgusted with him.
Major Bent is very well, and desires to be remembered to you. He is in a splendid position out
here. The weather is very hot—100° in the shade,
of which there is very little. General Dacres has
gone to Constantinople for a fortnight. A good
many French troops are being landed, and it is
said our allied armies amount to 165,000 men.
This is very tolerable ! I enclose a button cut off
from the coat of one of the Russians killed in our
trenches the other night. They are apparently
hard up for buttons.

Camp, June 1, 1855.—I neglected to write last
week, and am afraid I cannot communicate much
this. The Sardinians, French, and Turks have advanced into the plain of the Tchernaya, driven in

the Cossacks, and encamped on the ground the Turks lost at the battle of Balaclava. This enables us to extend our rides considerably over a beautiful country covered with thyme. I have been ordered to sketch it, so that I have not much time. We hear vague rumours of great doings at Kertch and elsewhere; but you must receive more intelligence than we do on this subject. The French, under their new general, Pellissier, have done some good work in front of the quarantine fort, where they have taken a long row of rifle-pits, and made them into a trench. We are on the eve of great events, and are ready to open fire at any minute. However, nothing certain is known yet.

Camp, June 8, 1855.—Nothing occurred of importance here until the 6th, beyond great activity in getting up our shot and shell, On the 6th, however, at three p.m., we opened fire from all our batteries. I was on duty in the trenches. I could distinctly see the Russians in the Redan and elsewhere running about in great haste and bringing up their gunners to the guns. They must have lost immensely, as our shot and shell continued to pour in upon them for hours without a lull. Never was our fire so successful. Before seven we had silenced a great many of their guns, while our loss was very small—only one man killed and four wounded. I was struck slightly with a stone from a round shot and stunned for a second, which old Jones has persisted in returning as wounded. However, I am all right; so do not think otherwise. Our fire was continued all night, and the next day until four o'clock, when we opened with new batteries much nearer, and our fire then became truly terrific. Fancy 1000 guns (which is the number of ourselves, the French, and Russians combined) firing at once shells in every direction. On our side alone we have thirty-nine 13″ mortars. At half-past five three rockets gave the signal for the French to attack the Mamelon and the redoubts of Selingkinsk and Volhynia. They rushed up the slope in full view of the allied armies. The Russians fired one or two guns when the French were in the embrasures. We then saw the Russians cut out on the other side and the French after them, towards the Malakoff tower, which they nearly reached, but were so punished by the guns of this work that they were obliged to retire, the Russians in their turn chasing them through the Mamelon into their own trenches.

This was dreadful, as it had to be assaulted

again. The French, however, did so immediately, and carried it splendidly. The redoubts of Volhynia and Selingkinsk were taken easily on our side. In front of the right attack a work called the Quarries had to be taken, which was done at the same time as the Mamelon. The Russians cut out and ran, while our men made their lodgment for our fellows. Lieutenant Lowry, R.E., was killed, and Anderson, a relation of the colonel, wounded slightly. We were attacked four times in the night, but held the work. If we had liked to assault, I am sure we should have taken the place with little loss, some of our men being close to the Redan. I do not know our exact loss, which of course would be rather heavy. If I find out before the mail closes I will tell you. I do not think the place can hold out another ten days; and once taken, the Crimea is ours. Henry saw it all, I believe; I sent him down word. Captain Dawson, R.E., was killed by a round shot in the morning of June 7th. Enderby left for Constantinople on the 6th, to bring up Turks to Kertch, where they have been doing wonders. The firing still goes on. The French took twenty guns and 400 prisoners, and found the Mamelon so traversed as to have no difficulty in making their lodgment.

We were driven from the Quarries three times in the night, the Russians having directed all their efforts against them. Four officers were killed and four wounded of the 88th Regiment. Our loss is supposed to be 1000 killed and wounded. Major Bayley, Captains Corbet and Wray, 88th, and Lieutenant Webb, killed. Nearly all our working party had to be taken for fighting purposes. The attacking columns were 200 strong; one went to the right, and the other to the left of the Quarries. The reserve consisted of 600 men. The Russians fought desperately. Once during the engagement the French succeeded in putting their scaling ladders against the round tower, but they could not maintain this advantage. Our loss in officers is twenty-seven killed and wounded. I send a rough plan, by which you may make out the places taken by our troops and the French.

Camp, June 12, 1855.—Although nothing to tell you, I write in case you should be anxious. Our fire slackened to-day, in order to let the French finish their battery on the Mamelon. All the Russian ships have moved out into the middle of the harbour, where we hope soon to touch them up. I am in great hopes that ten days will finish this siege. We had an armistice to bury the dead on the 10th, when the Russians appeared very down-hearted; no wonder, after their losses. The Russian works are simply ruined by our fire.*

Camp, June 15, 1855.—We are still, as you see, *before Sebastopol,* but (D.V.) it will not be for long. I will mention one thing I want you to get me, *if the place falls* (as you will hear it almost as soon as it does fall), viz. Jervois's map of the Crimea, the large one, and let me know what you pay for it. That is all I am in want of. . . . Some of the Kertch regiments have returned, and I believe Anderson is to remain there. We have held the Quarries, and made three approaches from them towards the Redan. I enclose a small sketch of them. The Russian ships of war are lying out in the harbour, as the redoubts taken by the French render their old position untenable. I hope you will apologize to my sisters for my not writing, but I really have no time. I think the Russians

* A friend who was in the siege has supplied the following note : —" Charley has had a miraculous escape. The day before yesterday he saw the smoke from an embrasure on his left, and heard a shell coming but did not see it. It struck the ground about five yards in front of him and burst, not touching him. If it had not burst it would have taken his head off."

seem down-hearted, although still determined. They are much to be admired, as they cannot have any great interest in the war. I believe, however, that quick promotion is their chief stimulant Henry will tell you that the Sardinians have advanced up the valley of the Baidar, where there is a small shooting-box in such a pretty place. The Russian officers are quite as cool under fire as our officers. A party of them were working at an embrasure in the Upper Town Battery. During the day we placed a 10″ gun to bear on them; for three shots they stood unmoved. The officer got on the parapet and waved his cap at every round. At the fifth shot, however, we sent them to the right about. In my opinion we shall begin firing again in three days, and then fire for thirty-six or forty-eight hours, and afterwards finish the siege, which may be the last of modern sieges according to the old rules. After the disastrous ending to their outworks, the Russians have since given up constructing new ones. You must know more of the Kertch expedition than we do here, although, as you may have heard, Mr. Russell, the *Times* correspondent, was refused leave to land. An old plan of the Russian works up to January last was found in the Mamelon.

Camp, June 21, 1855.—I must now commence
my long story of our attempted assault. To take
up my account from June 14, which was the last
letter I wrote to you. Seeley, my fellow-subaltern
at Pembroke, arrived on the 15th, and joined the
right attack. On the evening of the 16th it was
rumoured we were to commence firing again in the
morning. I was on duty on the morning of the
17th; and I went down at half-past two a.m. At
three a.m. all our batteries opened, and throughout
the day kept up a terrific fire. The Russians answered slowly, and after a time their guns almost
ceased. I mentioned in my report that I thought
they were reserving their fire. We did not lose many
men. I remained in the trenches until seven p.m.,
rather a long spell, and on coming up dined, and found
an order to be at the right attack at twelve, midnight,
on June 17 and 18. I was attached to Bent's column,
with Lieutenants Murray and Graham, R.E., and
we were to go into the Redan at the Russians' right
flank. Another column, under Captain de Moleyns
and Lieutenants Donnelly and James, R.E., was to
go in at the angle of the salient; and another, under
Captain Jesse, Lieutenants Fisher and Graves, was
to go in at the Russian left flank. We passed
along in our relative positions up to the advanced

trench, which is 200 yards from the Redan, where we halted until the signal for the attack should be given from the eight-gun battery, where Lord Raglan, Sir G. Brown, and General Jones were. About three a.m. the French advanced on the Malakoff tower in three columns, and ten minutes after this our signal was given. The Russians then opened with a fire of grape which was terrific. They mowed down our men in dozens, and the trenches, being confined, were crowded with men, who foolishly kept in them, instead of rushing over the parapet of our trenches, and, by coming forward in a mass, trusting to some of them at least being able to pass through untouched to the Redan, where, of course, once they arrived, the artillery could not reach them, and every yard nearer would have diminished the effect of the grape by giving it less space for spreading. We could then have moved up our supports and carried the place. Unfortunately, however, our men dribbled out of the ends of the trenches ten and twenty at a time, and as soon as they appeared they were cleared away. Some hundred men under Lieutenant Fisher got up to the abattis, but were not supported, and consequently had to retire. About this time the French were driven from the Malakoff tower, which

I do not think they actually entered, and Lord
Raglan very wisely would not renew the assault, as
the Redan could not be held with the Malakoff
tower in the hands of the Russians. Murray, poor
fellow, went out with the skirmishers of our
column, he in red and they in green. He was not
out a minute, when he was carried back with his
arm shattered with grape. Colonel Tylden called
for me and asked me to look after him, which I
did; and as I had a tourniquet in my pocket I put
it on. He bore it bravely, and I got a stretcher
and had him taken back. (I am glad to say that
Dr. Bent reports he did not die from loss of blood,
but from the shock, not being very strong. He
died three hours afterwards, and was, I am glad to
say, well prepared.)

A second after Murray had gone to the rear,
poor Tylden, struck by grape in the legs, was
carried back; and although very much depressed
in spirits, he is doing well. Jesse was killed at
the abattis, shot through the head; and Graves was
killed further in advance than any one. We now
sat still, waiting for orders, and the Russians
amusing themselves by shelling us from mortars.
When we appeared, the Russians lined their parapets as thick as possible, and seemed to be ex-

pecting us to come on. They flew two flags on
the Malakoff tower the whole time in defiance of
us. About ten o'clock some of the regiments got
orders to retire. We, the Royal Engineers, however, stayed until twelve o'clock, when we were
told that the assault was not to be renewed, and
that we could go. Thus ended our assault, of the
result of which we felt so sure. The first plan
made was that we should fire for three hours and
go in at six o'clock, but the French changed it, and
would not wait until we had silenced the enemy's
artillery fire; and so we attacked at three a.m. My
father can tell the effect of grape from twelve
68-prs and 32-prs. at 200 yards from a column; but,
whatever may be the effect, I am confident that if
we had left the trenches in a mass some of us would
have survived and reached the Redan, which, once
reached, the Highland Brigade and Guards would
have carried all before them, and the place would
have fallen. General Jones was struck by a stone
in the forehead, but not much hurt. I believe it
is said that the trenches were too high to get over.
As the scaling ladders were carried over them, this
can hardly be sustained. So much for *our* assault.
Now for the assault which was made from the left
attack. General Eyre had an order given him to

E

make a feint at the head of the creek, if we were successful at the Redan; however, at five o'clock, when we had failed at the Redan, we heard a very sharp attack on the head of the creek. The 44th and other regiments advanced, drove the Russians out of a rifle-pit they held near the cemetery, and entered some houses there. The Russians then opened a tremendous fire on the houses, and the men took shelter in line, being under no command, their own officers not knowing where they were to go, or anything about the place, and no Engineer officer being with them. The men sheltered themselves in the houses until they were knocked about their ears. They then remained in different places, in fact wherever they could get any shelter, until dusk, as, if they had attempted to retire, they would have been all destroyed. . . . The men of General Eyre's column found lots of drink in the houses. Our losses in the four columns are 1400 killed and wounded, 64 officers wounded, and 16 killed. The French lost 6000 killed and wounded, they say! Nothing has occurred since the assault, but it is determined to work forward by sap and mine. . . . I have no wish to join the Mounted Engineers!

Camp, before Sebastopol, June 30, 1855.—First

for news. General Estcourt died last Sunday of
cholera, and Lord Raglan died on the evening of
the 28th, of wear and tear and general debility.
He is universally regretted, as he was so kind.
His body will be sent to England. I am really
very sorry for him. His life had been entirely
spent in the service of the country. Since our
failure we have done nothing but take ammunition
into the batteries. The French are making a new
battery to sink the ships if possible. I send you
some everlastings from the Mamelon and redoubts
near the Careening Bay, where the French failed on
February 22. There has been more fighting about
these spots than any other, as the long tumuli, or
mounds of dead, will show. The French do not
bury separately, as we do, but in great heaps. If
I can get any violets I will, but it is rather late in
the-year.

Camp, before Sebastopol, July 10, 1855.—I am
sorry to say that we still are not in the place, but
I hope we shall soon put an end to this siege.
Since I wrote, nothing much· has occurred. We
are making new batteries, and improving our old
ones. Captain A. Jordan was killed by a 13″ shell
in the right attack of July 5, and Major Harrison,

63rd, was killed riding to the trenches on the 7th. Lieutenant Graham, R.E.,* was rather severely wounded by stones from a round shot on Sunday night—a good deal cut in the face. We are pushing on our trenches towards the Redan, from which we are now distant 200 yards. The army in the field has advanced. I went to Lord Raglan's funeral procession with the fifty men of our corps, each corps having to send that number of men. Generals Simpson, La Marmora, Omar Pasha, and Pellissier were mourners. The body was taken on a gun-carriage to Kazatch, and from thence by the *Condor* to England. Pellissier put a wreath of the yellow everlastings on his coffin. I send you some dried specimens from the right and left attacks, where you would not walk if you did not want to be made a target of by the Rusks. Give my love to my mother, and thank her for her letter. Remember, in spite of all the absurd reports in the papers, that our troops never once passed the abattis in front of the Redan, which is sixty yards from it, and that we never have spiked a gun of the Russians. Lieutenant James, R.E., was taken prisoner by the Russians on July 5. He missed

* The present Major-General Sir Gerald Graham, V.C., K.C.B., the victor of Teb and Tamanieb.

his way, and walked into a Russian picket, who embraced him. We partially began firing again this morning. Some of the dried affairs * I enclose are from Balaclava.

Camp, before Sebastopol, July 21, 1855.—I have been dreadfully neglectful for the last ten days in not writing, but I really have been too busy, what with plans and other things, as all of our officers are sick, with few exceptions. Thank God, I keep uncommonly well. Poor Captain Mansell, 39th, was killed on the 11th by a shell. With this exception, and a small sortie with no result, nothing has taken place since I wrote. We lose a good many men in our batteries, but hope that in a short time our toils will be over, and we shall date from the town next winter. Many thanks for the map, which I got two or three days ago. The number of officers going home is very great. An attempt was made to burn the shipping the other day, by means of a small punt (like the one at London and Hungerford bridges, which a man pulls about, saying he has saved 100 men's lives), but it was discovered and chased. The French are making a battery on the Sapoune heights, which,

* General Gordon is referring to the everlastings.

I think, will polish off the ships. The effects of our fire next time will be crushing, as we have greatly increased our armament. My wants are few. A box of Rowland's odonto I will gladly accept. Nothing else, thank you. If we fail again, and have to stay the winter, I shall get underground, and be quite comfortable. We have now sick Gordon, Tylden, Brown, Hassard, Armit, Darrah, Somerville, Fisher (a nice fellow), Du Cane, Dumaresq, De Vere, Graham, and Cowell, Royal Engineers; and Jones and Wolseley,* Assistant Royal Engineers—a good list. I hope my father is well. Thank him very much for the map. I see Colonel Spencer frequently, and he is quite well. I was on duty with him last night. He has a very good hut, and seems very comfortable on Cathcart's hill. *July* 22.—I have just come back from General Dacres, who has not been very well.

Camp, before Sebastopol, Aug. 3, 1855.—General Dacres has left for a short time. He wanted change of air. The army is not very well at present; there is some fever about, but I think the weather and heat which produced the great sickness last year is past,

* The present Lord Wolseley, G.C.B.

and that, considering the quantity of animal matter, etc., lying about in the winter, it is quite astonishing how well we have kept. Colonel Yule, R.E., is out here amateuring; he is after blowing up those unfortunate ships. General Todleben, the Russian engineer, died three days ago; he is the man who has thwarted us for so long. He died from a wound received on the 18th, and through not taking care of it.* We shall notice his loss in the next attack we make, when, if it is well or even ordinarily well managed (as far as we can see), we shall get in. A fortnight or so will be near the time, in my opinion; although, in consequence of the change of commander-in-chief, we hear nothing of the intended moves. General Jones hangs out still, although not very well sometimes. There is a little disappointment at no mention having been made of Brown in the attack on the Quarries. I am tired of the inactivity, but when we move again, in advance or assault, it breaks the monotony. The Russians made a small sortie on the Woronzoff road, and broke our *chevaux de frize;* they then

---

* This was one of the false rumours so freely circulated in camps. General Todleben lived to take part in another famous siege, that of Plevna, where, however, he had to attack instead of defend.

retired. It is surprising what a lot of officers of ours are going away sick. I think we count nine on duty, and sixteen away sick in both attacks. Those who arrived in the summer have not stood well. Winter is the time to come out; the climate then is very like England. The Russians seem to be employing their energies on their second line of works. We have sent a shell through nearly every house in the town. The French are pushing up very close to the Malakoff, which does not like the proximity, and remonstrates with grape, etc.; but to no good. The loss of the French is, in killed and wounded, 100 per diem, ours about thirty in both attacks.

Camp, before Sebastopol, Aug. 10, 1855.—I am only going to write a short note this time, as positively nothing has occurred since my last. I think it likely that the French will try at the Malakoff tower in ten days or so, but do not think they wish for our assistance. If this does not succeed, I think the raising of the siege not very unlikely; but we know nothing. Montague, a captain of ours, was taken prisoner on March 22, and carried into the town. He has just been released, and is now doing duty here. They treated him very well, and even coolly showed him over the

Redan, which is, he says, much more formidable than it looks. Anderson has come back from Kertch. Montague says they, the Russians, are not hard-worked, and that all the shops were open when he was there; but that is two months ago. They bring down their ammunition and grub from Moscow. Simpharopol is not fortified, as we thought.

Camp, before Sebastopol, Aug. 17, 1855.—Although, as you will have heard, there has been an action * fought, I am afraid I cannot give you a description of it, as we, having expected an attack on the trenches for some time past, have always been kept there. I cannot make out whether the Russians meant a strong reconnaissance or a general action, which one would think they would have continued longer than this lasted. We opened fire this morning from all our batteries, and they are now catching it. I believe this opening fire is merely to support the French in their attack on the Malakoff, but do not know. The weather has got cooler again, which is a great advantage. I can give you no account of what we are going to do. I send you two things which may amuse you, but

* Referring to the Battle of the Tchernaya.

do not want them *exhibited*, viz. my tent's interior,
and a sketch of the Malakoff tower and Mamelon.
The Malakoff is quite a citadel. The French, however, made their way on June 18, over the lower
batteries, and got into those houses (see sketch) behind the Malakoff. My tent is dug out, and I
have put up my small patrol tent as a bed-curtain.
Have I not a magnificent pedestal? It nearly
fills my tent. The Russians brought, yesterday,
small bridgeways with them to enable them to
cross the river. I am afraid I cannot give you a
sketch of the field of battle, as I have not yet
been down there, but will try in my next. The
Sardinians behaved very well, I believe. I have
just heard that poor Oldfield, a captain of the Royal
Artillery, has been killed in the left attack by a shell
in the batteries. He was a capital officer, and, of
all men, deserved his promotion. Commander
Hammet, R.N., was also killed; this was in the right
or this attack. Major Henry, also a capital officer,
lost his arm at the shoulder in the left attack.
These, with two sappers and some gunners, are all
the casualities I know of as yet. The Russian fire
is slacker, but it may be pretence. I hear our
fire is to go on for three days, but do not know
what is to be done then. I hear that the French

took 1700 prisoners, which is a good number. The Russians were supposed to have large reserves in hand, in case of any success taking place, in which event they would have pushed on to Balaclava. Captain Hassard and Lieutenant Darrah, R.E., have both gone to England, also Colonel Gordon. Poor Colonel Tylden! He died on his way home, at Malta.

I want a new regulation forage cap of the old pattern, as I like them so much better than our new ones. Can you send me one out, and let me know *the price;* also three flannel shirts (blue, I think, is the best colour)? These are the only things I require as yet, but you must let me know the price. Colonel Harrison, R.A., I hear, is dead, at Scutari. . . . How very tired the Russians must be of being periodically hammered like they are! Our losses are always trivial to theirs during these bombardments. A great number of the Russians carry small copper crosses and prayer-books with them; but Montague says they are not devout. We have received an addition of four officers to fill up the places of the five we lost on June 17 and 18. . . . The Russians have just opened a salvo from all their batteries. It seems very odd. I suppose it is meant as a repayment for our taking them by surprise this morning. They certainly at this minute are very angry, and are expóstulating violently with their guns. It has stopped now a little. Our fire has not much effect in silencing their guns, as they have only to pull them out of the embrasures and put them behind their thick parapets, where nothing can touch them. Their town is now, in every part, under our fire; but their underground caves protect their men to a great degree. They have fired shot into, around, and over our camp, from guns placed or slung, as the guns were in the Baltic, at a high elevation of 35° or 40°. Two shot went within three yards of my pony, which, however, Government would have repaid. Colonel Norcott asks after the family very often. I am not ambitious, but what easily earned C.B.'s and majorities there have been in some cases, while men who have *earned* them, like poor Oldfield, got nothing. I am sorry for him. He was always squabbling about his batteries with us, but he got more done by his perseverance than any man before did. I am now obliged to conclude, but can tell you that this opening fire is only intended to reduce the fire from the place so that the Russians may not annoy us by shell or shot for a few days.

Camp, before Sebastopol, Aug. 25, 1855.—I have got accurate sketches done for you of Alma, the landing-place of the troops on September 14, last year, and shall try and get more of them if you like them. Poor Captain Belson, a friend of mine, died of fever on his passage to Scutari. I regret his loss very much. Our fire has ceased again after four days' continuance, and now we are still in uncertainty as to what is to be done. The Russians are making a bridge across the harbour, a very cool proceeding, but one which, I am sorry to say, we cannot interrupt. I think the French will go in at the Malakoff tower in a fortnight; they have been working up pretty close during our firing. I send you a small sketch of the Redan as it appeared after twenty-four hours' good hammering from our batteries. The number of mortar shell, 13″ and 10″, dropped into it per diem is something immense. One battery of eleven mortars plumps them in one after another, so that the Russians know that when one mortar is fired ten more are to follow. This must be very annoying, and I know what it is like from having experienced the nuisance of three Russian mortars firing one after another. When the 13″ shell drops in you see timber, platform, men, gabions, etc., all fly up in the air as if a mine had exploded.

The Redan looks very sickly, as we fire platoons of musketry all night to prevent the Russians repairing it, and give them shells all day. The Russians repay us by baskets of shells (about $5\frac{1}{2}''$), perhaps twelve at a time, each fired from a big mortar; it requires to be lively to get out of their way. The Malakoff tower is bullied in the same way as the Redan, but it is better able to stand it. The French burrow in the ground near the Malakoff, as it would require such a thick parapet to resist the shot at so near a proximity, so they excavate five feet below the surface. One of the 21st and one of the 42nd went over to the Russians the other day when we were expecting an attack from them, and, being prepared, I suppose they thought twice of coming out to attack us. What sketches do you want in particular? I shall send you one of our graveyards, with Graves' and all the other fellows' graves in it. What a consolation it will be to get the place! I have now been thirty-four times twenty hours in the trenches, more than a month straight on end. It gets tedious after a time; but if anything is going on, one does not mind.

We hear that the Russian loss at the battle of the Tchernaya amounted to 7000 or 8000 men. I have just received ——'s note, which I shall answer shortly in this. We pushed on about twenty yards nearer the Redan the other night, but from what I can hear it is not likely we shall assault that part of the Russian works again. I am sorry to say that General Jones has never got over his blow on the head; he has suffered from his liver, and is now feverish. I am afraid he will have to leave, when we shall have Lloyd up from Constantinople. General Dacres is still away; I do not know when he will return. . . . The Russian prisoners taken the other day seem to say that they are obliged to attack us, as they have no rations, and they also declare that their army is dispirited. From what I can hear, I imagine that if (as I do not think likely) we fail this next assault, we shall make some great effort and land at the Belbek, and try and invest from that side and take the place this year. The Russians thought they would succeed in their last sortie, as they brought gabions with them to intrench themselves. We found instructions on General Wrede, a Russian brigadier-general, in which he is directed to intrench himself on the hills, while Liprandi cut off the Baidar troops; and after that they were together to attack Balaclava.

Camp, before Sebastopol, Aug. 31, 1855.—There has not been much doing since I last wrote. The Russians, as I think I told you, have completed their bridge across the harbour, and hundreds cross daily, and carts also, so that there will not be much plunder. It is made of launches. At one o'clock in the morning of the 29th the large magazine in the Mamelon blew up while they were loading. It killed forty and wounded 120 men, besides one general and four other officers. The works are not much damaged by it. Twenty of our men were also wounded by the splinters, and one was killed. General Dacres returns in a few days. I dined with —— the other night, and while there my horrid pony broke loose with the saddle on. We could not find him until the next morning, when I got him again; and luckily he had not rolled on the saddle. I send by this mail a sketch of No. 3 mortar battery in the left attack, with Mr. Upton's house in the distance. Those mounds that you will observe are powder-magazines. . . . You might be interested, I thought, in it; the sketches want smoothing out. Tell me if you like my sending them to you; they are pretty accurate. If you like them, I will send more. The Russians still keep us on the *qui vive;* but they have not much chance, as we are quite awake to their endeavours, and have intrenched ourselves well on every side. How I should like a week in September partridge-shooting; it is very tedious here with nothing going on. The French still continue to sap on to the Malakoff. I expect the Russians have had almost enough of it, as their work must be very hard. Captain Du Cane has gone sick to Corfu. I send a sketch of the Mamelon. I know there is not a plan in England yet, as I had to make the plan for General Jones, and it has not yet gone home. My father may be interested about it; it will be a well-known place in after years. —— may make something of my daubs. I do not know if you think they are worth the postage. Nothing is going on. Many thanks for your letter, and the things when they arrive. You will see I had written to you for the shirts, so that I am very much obliged. I have just got some things out from ——, who has not sent the bill. I have written for it, as I intend to have no more. Captain Wolseley, 90th Regiment, an assistant Royal Engineer, has been slightly wounded with a stone. Brown is progressing favourably. I mess with Bent, but do not live with him.

F

Camp, before Sebastopol, Sept. 7, 1855.—I hope
by the time this arrives you will have received
the news of our having taken the south side of
Sebastopol, as we attempt it to-morrow, and I
think with better chance of success than last time.
We opened fire on the 5th, and have continued it
ever since. The French set fire to and burnt a
two-decker and a frigate. Captain Snow, of the
R.A., was killed yesterday. I have nothing more
to tell you until next mail, when (D.V.) I hope to
give you good news.

Sebastopol, Sept. 10, 1855.—We are at last in
possession of the vile place. The Russians set fire
to it and evacuated it on Saturday at midnight,
after having repulsed the English in the Redan,
and the French in the central bastion. However,
the French took the Malakoff, and the Russians,
fearing for their communications, cut. They have
left a great many guns, etc. Anderson is all right,
and Henry and Enderby also. We share in the guns,
etc., halves with the French. The Russians sank
all their ships, etc. Is it not glorious? I am
making a plan of the works with two other Royal
Engineers. We got into the Redan, but were
driven out again. Our loss is great. Colonel

Hancock, 97th, killed. We had three Royal Engineers wounded, none killed. . . . You will see everything by the papers; but I will write particulars next time, as this goes with the despatches. The conflagration and explosions were terrible; their strongest masonry forts were blown to atoms.

Camp,* Sebastopol, Sept. 16, 1855.—I must now endeavour to give you my idea of our operations from the eventful 8th of September to the present 16th. We knew on the 7th that it was intended that the French should assault the Malakoff tower at twelve the next day, and that we and another column of the French should attack the Redan and central bastion. The next day proved windy and dusty, and at ten o'clock began one of the most tremendous bombardments ever seen or heard. We had kept up a tolerable fire for the last four days, quite warm enough; but for two hours this tremendous fire, extending six miles, was maintained. At twelve the French rushed at the Malakoff, took it with ease, having caught the defenders in their bomb-proof houses, where they had gone to escape from the shells, etc. They found it difficult work

* General Gordon had been moved to the camp on the heights after the fall of the place.

to get round to the little Redan, as the Russians
had by that time got out of their holes. However,
the Malakoff was won, and the tricolour was hoisted
as a signal for our attack. Our men went forward
well, losing apparently few, put the ladders in the
ditch, and mounted on the salient of the Redan;
but though they stayed there five minutes or more,
they did not advance, and tremendous reserves
coming up drove them out. They retired well,
and without disorder, losing in all 150 officers, 2400
men killed and wounded. We should have carried
everything before us if the men had only advanced.
The French got driven back with great loss at the
central bastion, losing four general officers. They
did not enter the work. Thus, after a day of
intense excitement, we had only gained the Malakoff. Lieutenant Rankin, R.E., was with the ladders
and in the ditch of the Redan. Anderson was in
my old place with the working party. They did
not leave the trenches. It was determined that
night that the Highlanders should storm the Redan
the next morning. I was detailed for the trenches,
but during the night I heard terrible explosions,
and going down to the trenches at four a.m. I saw
a splendid sight, the whole town in flames, and
every now and then a terrific explosion. The rising

sun shining on the scene of destruction produced a beautiful effect. The last of the Russians were leaving the town over the bridge. All the three-deckers, etc., were sunk, the steamers alone remaining. Tons and tons of powder must have been blown up.

About eight o'clock I got an order to commence a plan of the works, for which purpose I went to the Redan, where a dreadful sight was presented. The dead were buried in the ditch, the Russians with the English, Mr. Wright reading the service over them. About ten o'clock Fort Paul was blown up—a beautiful sight. The town was not safe to be entered on account of the fire and the few Russians who still prowled about. The latter cut off the hands and feet of one Frenchman. They also caught and took away a sapper, who would go trying to plunder—for as to plunder, there was, and is, literally nothing but rubbish and fleas, the Russians having carried off everything else. I have got the lock and sight off a gun (which used to try and deposit its contents very often in my carcase, in which I am grateful to say it failed) for my father, and some other rubbish (a Russian cap, etc.) for you and my sisters. But you would be surprised at the extraordinary rarity of knick-knacks. They left their pictures in the churches, which form consequently the only spoil, and which I do not care about buying. I will do my best to get some better things if it is possible. On the 10th we got down to the docks, and a flag of truce came over to ask permission to take away their wounded from the hospital, which we had only found out that day contained 3000 wounded men. These unfortunate men had been for a day and a half without attendance. A fourth of them were dead, and the rest were in a bad way. I will not dwell any more on it, but could not imagine a more dreadful sight. We have now got into the town, the conflagration being out, and it seems quite strange to hear no firing. It has been a splendid city, and the harbour is magnificent. We have taken more than 4000 guns, destroyed their fleet, immense stores of provisions, ammunition, etc. (for from the explosions they did not appear to be short of it); and shall destroy the dockyard, forts, quays, barracks, storehouses, etc. For guns Woolwich is a joke to it. The town is strewn with our shell and shot, etc. We have traced voltaic wires to nearly every powder magazine in the place. What plucky troops they were! When you hear the details of the siege, you will be astonished. The length of the siege is nothing in comparison with our gain in having destroyed the place.

We are not certain what the Russians are doing on the north side, and as yet do not know whether we shall follow them up or not. We ought to, I think. It is glorious going over their horrid batteries which used to bully us so much. Their dodges were infinite. Most of their artillerymen, being sailors, were necessarily handy men, and had devised several ingenious modes of riveting which they found very necessary. There was a vineyard under our attack, a sort of neutral ground, where no one dared to venture, either Russian or English. We found lots of ripe grapes there. The Russians used to fire another description of grape into it. One night I was working with a party at this very spot, and out of 200 men, we lost thirty killed and wounded. We are engaged in clearing the roads, burning the rubbish, and deodorizing the town, taking account of the guns, etc. Nothing has transpired as to our future movements. Enderby and Henry are both well. 17th.—I hear Enderby is likely to go with General Dacres on the expedition which, it is said, is preparing to attack the north side.

Undated (end of Sept., 1855).—Only one line to thank you for your kind letter, and to say that I have really no time to write.   Anderson, R.E., has gone to Constantinople to hut the cavalry. Nothing is stirring; the Russians fire a little into the town.   We hear they are retreating, but do not believe it. . . . The French, it seems, took the Malakoff by surprise; they had learnt from a deserter that the Russians used to march one relief of men out of the place before the other came in, on account of the heavy fire; whilst this was being done the French rushed in and found the Malakoff empty.   The Russians made three attempts to re-take it, the last led by a large body of officers alone. Many thanks for your kind present, which I have not yet received.   I wish I could write more; to make up, however, I am collecting rubbish for you from the town. . . . Whenever the Russians com-menced a battery, they laid down first a line of wires to the magazine, with which they could blow it up at any time.   I enclose a small piece.

Oct. 3, 1855.—I send you and my father a present, which I hope you will like.   Do not *publish* my remarks, as they are only intended for your amuse-ment.   I leave this for some expedition to-morrow.

General Spencer commands. It is said there will be 4000 English and 4000 French troops. Bent is the commanding royal engineer; Nicholson, my captain, and another subaltern junior to me, and sixty sappers also accompany it. We do not know where we are going, but suspect it to be Nicholaieff. The whole of the fleet is also ordered to move with us. I will write you word whenever I know more. . . . Nicholaieff, I should add, is a large dockyard, which we want to burn.

S.S. Indian, Oct. 8, 1855.—We left Balaclava harbour on Saturday morning, and reached Kamiesch the same day. I saw Bent on board the *Royal Albert*, with General Spencer, who looks very well. We left Kamiesch at three o'clock on Sunday—a magnificent flotilla, upwards of eighty vessels. We are lucky in our vessel, and kept well up to the fleet. Nicholson is my captain, and there is another subaltern. We rendezvous five miles east of Odessa. I shall send this letter off by the first opportunity, so it is likely to end abruptly. We are 9000 * strong. I am very glad General Spencer is going. . . . *Oct.* 10.—We are now anchored off Odessa, and leave this evening for Kimburn, our destina-

* The English contingent had been augmented by 1000 men.

tion. It is a small fort on a narrow spit of land, and it is the intention of the navy to disembark us, and by that means cut off the garrison of this fort. I expect they will evacuate the place before we land.

Kimburn, Oct. 17, 1855.—We laid off Odessa from Monday the 8th, until Sunday the 14th, when we left for Kimburn fort, which we reached the same day about four o'clock. We could see the coast and fort quite distinctly. At seven o'clock, the first boat, with Giffard of the *Leopard,* and Hallwell, A.Q.M.G., landed and hoisted our flag. The coast is very flat, and is covered with sand-hills (no picks are required to dig it). I landed with the infantry about eight, and had been previously ordered to go forward with the skirmishers and occupy a village; but when we had advanced a distance of a mile, we saw the village was too much out of our line, so we didn't occupy it. There was no sign of an enemy. A few Arabs made a dash and got into the fort. The distance from shore to shore is one and a half miles—a large front—but General Spencer has placed the troops very well. The French take the left of us, and defend against sorties, etc. They are only 4000 strong. The country is flat all the way, with sand-hills! Our position is thus. We had agreed with the French only to make a *tête de pont*, but found afterwards that it was necessary to cut an indented line right across, and commenced the evening we landed, and by the middle of the next day had communicated from sea to sea. We have since strengthened it very much, and the French have made a second line. The sea was so rough the next day, that the fleet could do nothing. The mortar boats shelled them a little. We began to despair of the fleet, so the French engineers proposed to Bent to land him the Royal Engineer officers and sappers, and to open approaches against the place. He commenced that night, but the day turned out so smooth that the fleet went in, and after enduring a fearful fire for four hours the fort gave it up; 1200 prisoners, seventy guns (most of them disabled by our fire), and 200 killed. They are not the same style of soldiers as the Sebastopol men, these being young boys and old men. I have not been in the place yet, as I am busy with my plans. Of the sight presented by the fleet I can say nothing, as it was too magnificent. We have made small quick reconnaissances into the country, and see no foe, although we know 10,000 to be at Kherson. Geese, ducks, and swans, wild and tame, abound here. The sea is brackish, but there is no want of water. Of our future movements I know nothing. All are well whom you know, both Royal Artillery and Royal Engineers. We shall know to-day whether we still hold this line, or fall back on a shorter one, or advance. Fort Ostrakow might do for us, as it is high land. The terms of capitulation were—officers to keep their swords, and the men their baggage. The French take care of them.

P.S.—Two most awful explosions have just taken place at Fort Ostrakow, which they have blown up. We heard the shells, etc., exploding long afterwards.

Odessa, Oct. 14, 1855.*—We start from this to-day for Kimburn Fort. We have laid off this ever since Monday last, as the weather was not very good for landing. The telegraphs on land are working away, letting them know of our departure. We are proceeding along the coast, and the fleets look splendid. We expect to land to-morrow; but perhaps to-day, if it looks favourable. We are very lucky in our vessel, not too crowded. We anchored off Kimburn to-day at four o'clock, and perhaps

* This letter was written to another correspondent than the one to whom the preceding letter, describing the same event, was addressed.

GENERAL GORDON'S LETTERS.   77

will land to-morrow. *October* 15.—We landed
to-day at ten o'clock, and took the right of the
position, so as to defend it against any enemy
coming from Kherson. The French (who are
only 4000 strong, we being 5000) took the left,
to defend against the fort. The fort mounts sixty-
four guns, and is three miles from our landing-
place. *October* 16.—To-day was too rough for the
fleet to attack the fort. Last night we (the Royal
Engineers) had to commence the entrenching of the
whole line from sea to sea, the fort being on a long
spit or tongue of land, or rather sand, one and a
half miles across. *October* 17.—We completed our
entrenchment from sea to sea, and about ten o'clock
the fort was attacked by the fleet. Nothing can
give you an idea of the sight, as it is unexampled.
About two o'clock the fort gave in, after four hours'
most fearful bombardment, upwards of 800 guns
bearing upon it. We have got 1200 prisoners, guns,
etc., and move our position to-morrow (D.V.), as we
hear the Russian Imperial Guard are advancing
to the relief of the fort. We consequently expect
a battle almost any day; but, now we have entrenched our position, there is little to fear. I have
not been in the fort yet, as I am engaged finishing
our entrenchments, and write this description in a

great hurry. Spencer is well, and a *capital* general. I will write better in a day or two. All are well here.

Kimburn Fort, Oct. 26, 1855.—Although very busy, I will try to let you know what is going on here. We have been out on a reconnaissance for four days, and have seen nothing of the enemy. Only a few Cossacks presented themselves. The villages all round are quite deserted, and geese, ducks, etc., may be had for the killing. The English cavalry, with the quarter-master-general and myself, went to almost the end of the isthmus; we were met in the last village we went into by an old priest and some of the inhabitants in a great fright. We left them alone and returned. The French would have pillaged them and burnt their houses. All the villages around, with the stacks of hay, etc., have been burnt, and the country is quite a wilderness. The French and we ourselves have done this to prevent the Russians having any spot to stop at on their way down to this place. We are now engaged with the French in rebuilding the fort. They will leave a garrison of 3000 men here. The winter is very severe. Some of the windows in the fort have three sashes, and the sea is partially frozen during the winter. The country is very flat and swampy. The Czar was close here when the attack took place, and his last telegram to the governor was, " Remember holy Russia," which the Russian general did by getting drunk.

The engineer officer did not want to surrender. The French floating batteries worked well. One of them was hit sixty-four times, the shot only making an indent of two inches. Ostrakow was blown up, with two other batteries, a few hours after the capitulation. General Spencer is quite well, and is very kind. I hope he will get a division. The gun-boats wander about the Dnieper and Bug, but do not go up, as there are great batteries on both sides of those rivers. One general officer, forty other officers, 1384 men, 174 guns, nine 13″ mortars, and 25,000 shot and shell were taken. The Russians had 200 killed and wounded—not many, considering the fire. I hear that Lieutenant James, R.E.,* who was taken prisoner some time ago at Sebastopol, is in the fleet. I am very busy with plans, and will endeavour to send you a more coherent account when I have got them off my hands. I have

* General Gordon's subsequent companion on the Danube and in Armenia.

secured for you a pair of colonel's epaulettes and a
silver belt out of this fort, which I bought. . . . The
weather is good here ; not cold, but seasonable, and
I keep quite well, I am grateful to say, and I dare
say weigh a few pounds heavier than when I left
England.   You shall have a sketch of Kimburn as
soon as I have done the plans. . . . The *Illustrated
News* correspondent is here, sketching away, so his
sketches will give you some idea of the place.

Kamiesch, Nov. 2, 1855.—We have just anchored
here on our return from Kimburn, where the
French have left a garrison of 2500 men to hold
the fort, which we have repaired as well as we
could after the hammering it got. . . . Of course
I have heard no news yet from Sebastopol, but
see that the Russians still hold the north side, as
they are firing from it.   I expect you must be
sick and tired of the assault ; every one else is.
I will send you a sketch of Kimburn next mail.
We took a grand lot of prisoners, and from the
position of the fort, our possession of it will always
oblige them to keep large forces in the neighbourhood.   The country around is very flat.   It was very
good fun visiting the villages during the reconnaissance.   The people did not seem afflicted by the

fort being taken. Mind and go and see the prisoners. We had for our share the colonel and all the artillery officers. The French took the engineer and governor. We have not yet seen the *Gazette*, but I suppose shall do so to-day. I never want to see my old letters again.

Kamiesch, Nov. 4, 1855.—We are still here, not yet disembarked, as we expect to start off in a day or two for Kaffa and Arabat. I have just got your letter of the 18th of October. We shall have great changes here in our commander-in-chief. I believe General Simpson will go home at once, and General Eyre is likely to have the command. Sir Colin Campbell has left for England. Lady Dacres, I hear, is with General Dacres. I have not seen Enderby or Henry yet, as I have not had time to get out of the vessel; but I shall do so, to get some things, before we go to Kaffa. Nothing, by all accounts, appears to be going on in the Crimea. It is a great nuisance that General Jones has gone home, as he held a very high position, and always upheld us, and we do not know much of his successor. We have now been away from Sebastopol ever since the 2nd of October, and almost half that time has spent been on board ship. If we do go on to Kaffa, the whole of the 4th division will go, whereas now we have only one brigade. Have the Russian prisoners from Kimburn arrived yet? I met an old acquaintance here, who is a mate in one of the gun-boats, and who was at school with me in Somersetshire. The heavy brigade of cavalry have embarked for Scutari, and are to be wintered there. I do not think the Russians will leave the north side, but will try and delay us before it during the next campaign.

——* *Nov.* 18, 1855.—We have got the *Gazette* at last, and think they have treated us very well, and been very liberal. We landed from the *Indian* a week ago, the expedition to Kaffa, after a delay of a fortnight, being deferred to another time. We had a dreadful explosion in the French right siege train the other day. An enormous quantity of powder, shells, etc., blew up, and caused great destruction of property. The loss on our side was fifty-one casualties; I do not know the loss of the French. The shells kept on exploding for a considerable time. Lieutenant Dawson, R.A., lost his foot by a splinter; Lieutenant Roberts got his arm

* Not addressed from any place in particular, but bears internal evidence of having been written from the Camp at Sebastopol.

hurt. A Mr. Yolland, a commissary in the Field Train, was killed. Many thanks for the caps and for the Etna and cherry brandy. The Etna is a capital thing. I am now quite fitted for the winter, and require nothing more. I shall endeavour to send home my Sebastopol and Kimburn trophies soon, but plans, etc., take up nearly all my time. Henry is very busy. I have got a capital hut now, and am as well off as I should be in England. The weather looks fine, and the country is very dry. I have not received the shirts yet. I want my father to get me the enclosed articles and send them out as soon as possible; they are for my field sketching. I am sorry I cannot send a sketch of Kimburn yet, but will not forget it. . . . Nearly all the cavalry have gone to Scutari.

Dockyard, Sebastopol, Dec. 4, 1855.—I am now, as you see, stationed in the dockyard, preparing the shafts and galleries for the demolition of the docks. The French will destroy one half, and ourselves the other. The quantity of powder we shall use is 45,000 lbs., in charges varying from 80 lbs. to 8000 lbs. The French do not sink their shafts so deep as we do, but use heavier charges. The docks are very well made, and the gates alone cost £23,000. We are taking one gate to London, and the French another to Paris. Our shafts are some of them very deep, and in others there is from eight to ten feet of water. I shall send home my old regulation cap, and make ——, the tailor, exchange it for a new regulation cap. I shall enclose it to you, if you would kindly forward it to ——, and send me out the other one. This reminds me, that the box of *rubbish*, as I call these knick-knacks, went on November 24th, in the *Thames*, so that you will receive it near Christmas. There is not much prospect of the Russians leaving the north side. We can see them hutting themselves. The weather is changeable; sometimes snow, sometimes rain, but always wind. We have now got locomotives on the line, which is a great improvement.

Sebastopol, Dockyard, Dec. 27, 1855.—Very many thanks for your kind letter, and happy Christmas to you all. The weather here is very seasonable, and all the army seems healthy, and is both well fed and well clothed. It is a great nuisance about my shirts ; but I can get others very well out here. Pray do not think of sending me anything more, with the sole exception of the sketching-blocks and the new regulation cap. I send the old one home.

Our works at the docks approach completion, and we hope to blow up some portion of them on Saturday next. The French blew up one last Saturday. The explosion presented a splendid appearance, and succeeded admirably, not a stone being left standing. The powder for our demolition will be upwards of twenty-two tons. The Russians still hold the north forts, and do not appear to be likely to leave this year, as their huts are all built. We can see them quite distinctly on the other side. Have the *trophies* arrived yet? they ought to have done so by this. The mails have been very disappointing lately, never coming in in time. Did you notice a sketch of a house in the Karabelnaia suburb, where the mixed commission lived, in the *Illustrated London News?* We are now living in that house, and are very comfortable.

Sebastopol, Jan. 20, 1856.—You seem to imagine that I am perfectly threadbare and destitute, which at the best is not complimentary. However, I assure you I am very well off in every way. We have blown up part of our docks, and are very busy with the remainder, which we hope to get over by the end of the month. I do not anticipate any movement of the army until March, when I

suppose we shall go to Asia, to relieve Kars, and
make the Russians retire from the Turkish territory. I saw a letter from Anderson yesterday.
He is still at Scutari. He says Simmons, a colonel
of ours who was with Omar Pasha, has gone home.
There is no news at all here; and I do not
anticipate anything likely to break the monotony.
Remember, I do not think it is a hard case that
we, the subs., do not get anything.

Sebastopol, Dockyard, Feb. 3, 1856.—We all of us
have been extremely busy in loading and firing our
mines in the docks, which required all our time,
as we were so very short of officers, having only
three, while the French had twelve. Our force
of sappers was only 150, and the French had 600.
We have now finished the demolition, which is
satisfactory, as far as the effects produced are concerned; but, having used the voltaic battery instead
of the old-fashioned hose, we have found that
electricity will not succeed in large operations like
this, and I do not think that any one will use it, if
there is a possibility of using hose. I am now
engaged in making plans of the docks, and have
not much time to myself. The French have done
their work very well, using more powder than we,

and firing all their mines with hose. I will try and get you a photograph of the docks as they *were* and as they *are*, which will tell you more than a dozen letters would. We had an alarm down here the other night about twelve o'clock. The Russians on the north side opened a tremendous fire throughout their whole line on us and on the French. We were all out under arms, expecting an attack by boats, but after being well shelled for an hour, the Russians left off, and all was again silent; but, for the time it lasted, the fire was terrific.

I heard afterwards that it was caused by a French navy captain, who pulled over to the other side of the harbour, and tried to burn a steamer, which was lying on its side. He and his companions arrived unperceived, found the steamer quite new, and were getting into it, when the Russian sentinel challenged. They answered "Russe," but the sentry called "to arms," and the Russians fired into the boat, and then continued the fire from all their guns, I suppose expecting a grand attack. Only one man, however, was hurt by a splinter on the arm. The French will blow up Fort Nicholas on Monday. They only got their order the night before last, and are obliged to make a hasty demolition of it. They will use 105,000 lbs.

of powder in the demolition. The Russians had mined this fort, but had not had time to put the powder in; the excavations were complete. Their shafts were seven feet deep and galleries five feet long under each pier. The French will put their charges of 2500 lbs. each in every alternate ground casement and tamp up all orifices. They will fire it with hose. It certainly is a splendid fort, mounting 128 guns, and capitally finished for barracks. It would hold 6000 men. The Russians evidently intended this to be an exceptionally strong place, and they appear to have been making a quay all the way round the dockyard creek. I mean to send you home a lot more photographs when I can get them. What a splendid thing photography is! It is so accurate, and tells the truth so much better than any letter.

We have used 50,000 lbs. in the destruction of the docks; the French rather more. The French lost 100,000 lbs. in their great explosion at the windmill on November 15. We have seen a great deal of the French engineers; they are older men than ours, and seem well educated. The non-commissioned officers are much more intelligent than our men. With us, although our men are not stupid, the officers have to do a good deal of work

which the French sapper non-commissioned officer
does. They all understand line of least resistance, etc., and what they are about. They cal-
culate their charges differently; thus b represents
the line of least resistance in metres; b^3 gives the
charge in kilogrammes for earth; $4b^3$ gives the
charge in kilogrammes for masonry. This will
give a much larger charge than our calculation.
The French tried the effect of a charge of 1600 lbs.
of powder placed in a tank on the masonry bottom
of one of their locks, with seventeen feet of water
over it, and fired it by galvanic battery. It produced a hole 7 ft. 6 in. deep in the masonry, and shook
the sides of the lock very much. We have taken
one gate down, and I believe it will be sent to
London, for one of the parks. The Russians do not
molest us much now. We can hear them call out
and sing, especially on Sundays. We see them
drill, which they do every day. They even have
the coolness to go out and fish in the harbour. We
never fire; neither do the French. I do not think
they purpose leaving the north side; in fact, it
would not be at all wise of them to do so. We had
a sad accident the other day in one of our mines.
The men went down too soon after the firing of
some adjacent mines, and the gallery was full of

gas (carbonized oxide). We got the men out as soon as possible, but one was dead before he could be reached. It is an odd occurrence, as the gallery was fifty feet from the other mine, but the earth is very porous. . . . I suppose we shall move up to camp again in a short time, unless we have any more demolitions to undertake. I am dreadfully in debt as to letter-writing, and I do not see how I shall pay it off, as my whole time is taken up with plans.

——* *Feb.* 22, 1856.—I am a dreadful fellow, never to have written to you for so long ; but there really is not much news, and I have a great deal to do. We are now engaged in getting ready for the spring campaign, and shall make a defensive position around Balaclava, so that we may be able to disembark if peace should turn out to be humbug. Major Cooke, R.E., is looking out for fossils for Colonel James ; we found some the other day. We have had very cold weather for the last day or two, the thermometer down to 10° ; but to-day it is quite warm again. We had seven French engineers to dine with us the other day ; they were very agreeable, and we learnt a great deal from them about

* No place given.

their mining. They used to hear the Russians mining within ten feet of them, and when they did this they used to put in their powder as quick as possible and blow in the Russian mines. The Russians had two systems or layers of mines, one about ten feet below the surface of the ground, and the other about forty feet. The French only knew of the higher one, and they found out after the place was taken that their advanced trenches were quite mined and loaded in the lower tier. In the Bastion du Mât there were no less than thirty-six mines loaded and tamped. I saw one myself in the upper tier, when I was surveying it. They (the Russians) worked out a strata of clay between two layers of rock, so that no wood was required to keep the earth from falling in. . . . Is there anything I can get you in the way of relics, or as I call them, rubbish ? Let me know.

Camp, near Sebastopol, March 9, 1856.—We have, as you have seen, finished the docks, plans and all. We had a sad accident the other day. An officer of ours, Major Rankin, was setting light to a set of mines under the wall of the White Barracks, and it is supposed the fuse was bad, as, instead of its burning as long as it ought to enable him to get away, the charges of powder went off instantaneously, and he was buried in the ruins. We got his body out after considerable trouble. He had got his majority and company about two months ago. It is very sad, as he was the engineer who went with the ladders on September 8. I have heard and seen nothing of the sketching-blocks. It seems as if I were to be unfortunate in my parcels. We have still got snow, and the thermometer is very low. This, after we have had crocuses, etc., is exceedingly odd. I have just got your letter of February 21, and will answer it by this. I really am quite tired of the flannel shirt question. It has been going on for nearly six months. I am very well supplied in every way. We do not, generally speaking, like the thoughts of peace until after another campaign. I shall not go to England, but expect I shall remain abroad for three or four years, which, *individually*, I would sooner spend in war than peace. There is something indescribably exciting in the former. We have not signed an armistice yet, but a truce, which may be broken off at any time. The French are suffering a good deal from scurvy and bad food. Whether this is from want of money or transport we do not know. I must say this climate is marvellous and eccentric; to-day it is quite like

summer. Our army is in splendid condition, and
Sir Wm. Codrington is very well liked.

—— * *March* 21, 1856.—I have just received the
packet of drawing-boards, for which I am much
obliged, and also my new cap from ——, so that I am
now complete and shall not require anything more.
The weather here is still very cold, and very different from what we had last year. The truce still continues, and the Russians make a good business out
of selling crosses and other things to our officers.
The river Tchernaya forms the boundary of our
ground. The Russians have been across, even up
to the top of Inkerman. There are still the remains
of men and horses who were killed in that battle ;
they are quite skeletons now. There are to be, on
Monday next, some horse-races in the valley of
the Tchernaya, where the battle of Traktir took
place. It is a beautiful valley, with very high
mountains to the east of it. The French out
here have got their Crimean medal and wear it.
Russell, the *Times* correspondent, has come back. I
shall be very glad to move from here ; it is now
nearly fifteen months that we have been in the same
spot. We have got up a mess, which is a great

* No place named.

advantage. I saw Colonel Marriott the other day; he desired to be remembered. Will you tell my father that the sights come off the middle of the guns, where the Russians always put them, and the guns were 40-prs. or 42-prs. ? I have lost his note, but I think that was all he asked. Have you seen or heard anything of Sir H. Jones ? I have sent for some more photographs, but they have not yet arrived; they are now to be got in London for ten shillings apiece. Fenton has an exhibition in London which I believe is well worth seeing. The Russians on September 8 brought a field battery up against the Malakoff, but on their retreating, they drove the battery, horses and all, into the sea, over the wharf. We have now got a diving-dress, and sent a man down to get the guns up, and succeeded in getting up one. We do not hear anything about the peace movements.

Sebastopol, April 25, 1856.—We have, as far as our corps is concerned, heard nothing of our future destination. However, I think I shall remain abroad, as there is not much allurement in the home duties of our people, and I should not go on the survey, *even* if I had the offer. The 9th, 17th, 39th, 62nd, and 63rd regiments leave, under General

Eyre, for Canada to-morrow, and it is believed that
six regiments will soon be detailed for India.   The
two batteries of artillery, which were stopped at
Constantinople a fortnight ago, will also go.   If
there is anything to be *done* in Canada, we should
go from here *en masse*, so that peace would only
change the scene.   We certainly have got a splendid
army here — upwards of 28,000 infantry — and
I equipped with everything needful for a campaign.
am sorry to hear about the medals, as there will be
no end to them.   I visited the field of Alma yesterday; it is a fifty-mile ride there and back, over a
grass country quite unlike this side, and completely
deserted.   There are not many marks of the battle
beyond the battery, which the 23rd Regiment carried.
The sketch is very good which I sent you; I recog-
nized it in a minute.   There are not many villages
about.   The north side is strong, but the North or
Star Fort is a tumbledown affair, and not at all
formidable.   Fort Constantine is well built, and has
suffered very little by the fire of the shipping on
October 17. They told us that they could not
fight the guns on the top after the first two hours,
but that the guns in casemate were serviceable
until the last.   There were seven guns disabled
lying in the courtyard.   The photograph man has

not come up yet, but I shall not forget when he
comes. The Sardinian army is embarking daily,
and I heard that the French had evacuated Kimburn and Eupatoria. The Russians live in a filthy
state, and keep their camps in the same. You can
detect them a mile off. The officers speak a little
French or German, but are not so wonderfully
educated as one hears. Suders, the Russian general,
reviewed us and the French army last week. He
must have thought our making peace odd.

Camp, before Sebastopol, May 10, 1856.—I have
been up the country for three days, and had a
delightful time of it. The south coast is quite a
garden, the Woronzoff road passes through vineyards and orchards for miles, and after the arid
view one has here, it is quite a relief. There are
no signs of war there, although so near this, the
only troops being Cossacks, who, however, maltreat
the poor Tartars. There are a great many palaces
along the coast; the finest, at Aloupka, belongs to
Prince Woronzoff, and was built and designed by
an Englishman. It is something like Windsor, and
is beautifully situated. There is the Empress's
palace at Onianda, which is also well worth seeing.
All these palaces are furnished, and the owners

are expected down this year. When the French advanced to the Baidar Valley, they used to make forays into these chateaux. The Tartars who lived at Baidar and the other villages about here, and who gave us any assistance they could, have been removed to Constantinople, as the Russians have been heard to say that they would hang them. Colonel Gordon, R.E., has left for Jerusalem on leave; Colonel Stanton, R.E., has gone to Bessarabia to settle the boundary; and Colonel Simmons has proceeded to Asia Minor for the same purpose. Several regiments have left for Canada, but no more are to go until all the Sardinians have left. But I believe that there are enough vessels to take them all at once. We have not heard a word about our destinations, but shall, I suppose, next mail. The French leave daily. I shall be able to get the photographs of the destroyed docks next week. General Spencer left yesterday for England. He has been very kind to me. It will be a great shame if he does not get made a major-general. My servant, a Tartar, and Anderson's servant, a Turk, took our horses down to get grass, and, being of an inquiring mind, put a match on top of the fuze of an unexploded shell which had been fired during the siege. The shell went

H

off, to their surprise, and blew off Anderson's servant's thumb, and burnt the hair off the head of my servant. It is quite extraordinary that it did not kill them both, and in nine cases out of ten it would have done so. We have picked up 150,000 shot, which had been fired at the English alone, in the ravines, etc. We are not allowed to take our horses home, so we shall have to give them away, as it is impossible to find buyers for so many. Is there anything you want while I am out here?

P.S.—I have just received my orders to join Stanton in Bessarabia, and shall leave this to-day. I will write again soon.

Constantinople, May 18, 1856.—I received your letter of May 2 to-day; but, as you will know by my last letter, I have left the Crimea *en route* to join Stanton in Bessarabia, to trace the new frontier line. We arrived here on the 16th, and believe that we leave this by the Lloyds mail packet on the 20th, which will take us to Galatz. I imagine the work will occupy about six months, as the new line is 100 miles in length. . . . The Ramazan or Great Fast is going on here, and the mosques are lit up at night. We visited St. Sophia last night, and got in, but with some difficulty. It is somewhat like St. Paul's inside but is more emblazoned. The Sultan, they say, is in great fear of disturbances in his dominions, and has issued a firman threatening to ask for the aid of foreign troops. The Turkish contingent is being disbanded, and the officers get two months' pay for a reward, and £30 for their chargers in lieu of taking them home. I have left word for the photographs of the destroyed docks to be sent to my father as soon as they are printed. I will write again from Galatz, and once a week afterwards.

PART II.

LETTERS FROM THE DANUBE.

General Note on the Danubian Question by General Gordon.

At the Paris Congress in 1856, it was determined to eloign the Russians from the Danube and its tributary lakes and streams. The Powers therefore stated that the frontier should pass south of Bolgrad, judging from the small scale map supplied by the Russians that Bolgrad was north of the Lake Yalpukh, which opens into the river Danube. When the Boundary Commission came on the ground, they found that Bolgrad was on the Lake Yalpukh, and that if the frontier passed to the south of it the Russians would have access to the river Danube ; and therefore, knowing the spirit of the treaty, the English commissioner referred the question to the Paris Congress. Our sketch was prepared to show the diplomatists its exact position, and led to the frontier being laid down north of Bolgrad, and of the Lake Yalpukh.

Galatz, May 23, 1856.—We arrived this morning, after three days' voyage from Constantinople, having visited Varna on our way. Varna is a lonely Turkish town, and only interesting from the fact of our troops having left for the Crimea from it. The steamer, which was one of Lloyds' Austrian packets, kept close to the shore all the way. The coast is pretty, but looks quite uninhabited. The mouth of the Danube (Sulina) is not a quarter of a mile broad, and there are the wrecks of twenty vessels lying there. The sand-bar has only ten feet of water over it, although the Russians engaged to keep it clear. From the mouth of the Danube to Tulscha the river is exactly like the Thames at Barking Reach, nothing but reeds, and a dead flat. A little above Tulscha the Kilia branch, which runs to Ismail, commences. This is the point where Suders crossed in the beginning of the war, with 45,000 men. It is about 600 yards broad. The Russian pickets are along one shore, and the Turks along the other. The Russian commissioner has objected to the Moldavian com-

missioner, as he says that he is not mentioned in
the treaty as being one of the commissioners for
the new boundary; but we think this is only to
gain time. However, that question will be settled
in a day or two. There is a French colonel for
France, a Russian general for Russia, and an
Austrian general for Austria. I have only seen
the French commissioner as yet. We are to go
along the boundary, and compare the country
with the Russian maps. If these are incorrect,
we, i.e. James and myself, will have to survey it.
I cannot yet tell you the exact boundary or much
more about it, but will do so as soon as I can find
out. Galatz is very dusty, and not at all a de-
sirable place of residence. The inhabitants are
28,000. There is an Austrian garrison here, and
there are also the Moldavian militia, who are
dressed exactly like the Russian soldiers. We came
up in the steamer with some Austrian officers. It
is a ludicrous thing to observe how they despise
the Russians; but so they pretend at least to
do. Will you send all letters for me to the care
of the British consul at Galatz? Moldavia appears
to consist of low ground with undulating hills.
The prices here are very low; meat twopence and
threepence per pound, and corn equally cheap.

Mind and tell —— that I have heaps of quinine, or I shall have it sent out.

Bolgrad, June 9, 1856.—We arrived here yesterday, having left Galatz on June 7, and slept in a village on the road. We crossed the Pruth near Reni. It is about forty yards broad, and has a good current; but much above Reni there is scarcely any navigation. The Russians are uncommonly civil. It would have made you laugh to see the way the people crowded about us, almost as if we were wild beasts. I met some Sebastopol Russian officers here; they were also very civil. The country between this and Reni is very flat, with slight ravines, and is about 160 feet above the sea. It is sown with corn in large tracts, which seem endless, as there are no hedges or trees, but only a level plain. There are a few villages in the bottoms of the ravines, where water is to be found. On our way here, I met an emigration of "hoppers," *i.e.* young locusts before they get their wings. The ground was quite black with them, and there were several parties of eighty to one hundred men and boys, with pieces of cloth tied to sticks, extended in line across these large tracts of country, and endeavouring to drive the hoppers towards the road, where they fall into a trench cut for the purpose, and which stops their career. As they fall into it, it is filled up. This is, of course, a very inefficient mode of getting rid of them.

Corn is very cheap here, and the amount of land is so great that the same tract is only cultivated once in five years, and by that means they avoid the trouble of manuring or ploughing deep. There is a great want of water in every part except in the ravines. Bolgrad is a largish place, and the head-quarters of the Bessarabian army. The Volhynian regiment, which made the second redoubt on the Sapoune heights at Sebastopol is here, or, rather, it is at this very moment at Ismail, destroying the works, etc. It left the Crimea on December 7, and arrived here on January 29, 1856, a march of two months nearly, in the winter. What losses they must have suffered! We leave this in a few days for Katamori to reconnoitre the ground, but still direct to the English Consul at Galatz, as the letters are to be sent on there. The way we are put up is by turning the people out of part of their houses, which are given over to us. They do not mind, as they are paid pretty well by us. There are four Cossacks told off to attend on and accompany us. Very likely a little espionage is mixed up with the compliment; but they are, certainly, more civil than the Austrians. I do not think I have any more to say at present, but shall leave this letter open for a few days. Bolgrad is marked Tabor on the map ; it is on Lake Yalpukh. *June* 16.—We leave this to-morrow for the Pruth (Katamori).

Kartaleni, ten miles from Pruth, June 29, 1856. —We left Bolgrad on June 18, and by short journeys of twenty miles per diem arrived at this place, which is a small village near the Pruth, and about eighteen miles from Katamori, the extreme western point of the boundary. We usually start at four in the morning, and get the journey over by the beginning of the hot part of the day. There are in each village (which are miserable enough) houses told off for each commissioner; but I generally sleep in my tent, as it is cleaner. From Seratzika, which is at the source of the Pruth, I went to Kichenau, the capital of Bessarabia, to get provisions, etc. It is a place with nothing of interest about it. There was one regiment of cavalry in it. A person can travel about very cheaply here. I paid, for eighty miles, something under £1 for three horses (posting). The vehicles are very bad, being nothing more than small arabas. There are pelicans, bustards, large and small, and hares and partridges here. The country is better than at Bolgrad; the hills are higher, and there is more wood. It is the same style of prairie country. We *may* finish by the end of October, but I doubt it, as the Russians are just the same as they usually are, finding many difficulties in nothing. Stanton and the French colonel, Besson, and myself feed together. The Frenchman has no one else with him. Our sappers and James are at Bolgrad. We shall return to-morrow to Seratzika, and I shall go from there to Kichenau, and from Kichenau by the Pruth to Jassy, to take the despatches. Stanton goes on to Bolgrad. I shall leave this letter until I arrive at Jassy.

I left Destindje on Tuesday morning at five o'clock, June 30, and passing through Leovo, Husch, and Vuslion, arrived at Jassy, after a wet ride, at half-past two on July 1. I travelled in post cars, a species of low-wheeled truck without springs, very light and quite open, which bump along the roads at a good rate with four horses. Through the rain, I was in a precious mess. I got on pretty well, not knowing one word of the language. I lost a wheel once. Jassy I like very much. The

people were very civil, and asked me about a great
deal. I was taken to visit the Hospodar, Prince
Ghika, who was also very civil. The ladies and
gentlemen are very political at present about the
union of the principalities under a foreign prince.
The town is pretty, but living is much more ex-
pensive than in London. The boyars live away
most part of their lives at Paris, and the society
is quite French. There are about 30,000 Jews in
Jassy, who live upon these boyars, asking 200 per
cent. The crops promise to be extraordinarily fine
this year. I went to Jassy with despatches, and
to bring back a cypher to Stanton. I stayed there
three days. The prince keeps up a great state, and
I was introduced to him with much ceremony. The
English uniform produces an immense sensation.
Four Russians were shot the other day for murder.
The Austrian general Parr, to whom I paid a visit,
is now very strict. I left Jassy in a carriage,
which I had bought for Stanton, in pouring rain
on Saturday night, and arrived at Galatz on Monday
morning, travelling incessantly night and morning,
with six to eight horses each ten miles. I stopped
at Galatz two hours, and then started for Bolgrad,
which I reached at nine o'clock at night, and where
I found that the commission was to start next day

to accomplish the remainder of the frontier to the Black Sea. I met a lot of people at Jassy, nearly all titled. One of them, the best, was a Russian colonel of Cossacks, a Prince Wittgenstein,* who distinguished himself very much at Kars. He met and married a Moldavian lady at Paris, and is a very nice person.

Akermann, mouth of the Dniester, July 17, 1856. —We have now been over the whole of the frontier, from Katomori on the Pruth, to Boma Sola on the Black Sea, a distance of very nearly 200 miles. It is an odd sort of life, going about twenty miles per diem, and camping for the day about ten o'clock; but the country wants trees to make it pretty. It has not been very hot, and as yet we can complain of no want of rain, having had not merely thunderstorms, but Irish rain for whole days at a stretch. The shooting here will be good in the proper season, as there are lots of bustards and other animals. As for its being unhealthy, it is a mistake, as we are never nearer the Danube than eighty miles, and it is only the decayed vegetation of that river which causes fever at Galatz,

* A member of this family, Prince Victor Wittgenstein, served afterwards in China with General Gordon against the Taepings.

Bucharest, and Giurgevo. The land we travel on is
quite dry, being about 250 feet above the sea, and
is far, indeed, from being marsh land. Akermann
is a town (Russian) of 30,000 people, and, like all
Russian towns, is at a standstill. There is an old
Turkish fort here. The country around is very
sandy, and not at all low, as the maps lead one
to suppose. The other side of the estuary of the
Dniester is the same. We are now finally deciding
the frontier on *the maps*, and when this is done, we
shall mark on the *ground itself* the posts of the new
frontier. I do not think we shall be more than two
and a half months longer. As far as this place,
everything has gone on very well, and I like the
work extremely. I shall go to Odessa in a few
days, and will let you know what I think of it.
—— wants me to bring home a Russian wife, I
think; but I am sure you would not admire the
Russian ladies that I have seen. I shall not write
to Henry until I hear of his arrival in England, as
it is useless sending to the Crimea. Let me know
any reports about our corps' proceedings that you
can pick up; particularly as to whether we are
likely to be reorganized, or whether a separation
will take place between the civil and military parts
of our corps; as, if there is such a change, I shall

certainly try for the latter. Let me know if you hear anything of a staff corps being formed.

General Codrington was at Odessa a few days ago, on his way home. The Jews swarm here. In fact, I am sure they compose the greater part of the population. They wear a long coat, and are very strict about their sabbath on Saturday, which is a great trouble to us, as we have three Jewish drivers who always want to stand still on that day. There is a colony of Swiss emigrants near here; they have been here thirty years, and have done a great deal of good to this place. The Russians encourage these immigrants in every possible way; they have German, French, Swiss, Bulgarian, and Cossack colonies. The last are very peculiar; the men at fifteen years are made soldier Cossacks, which they remain for three years; they then go back to their village for three years; after that, another three years of military service, and so on, until they complete twenty-one years' military service, when they return to their village for the rest of their life. The original Russian is a very rare thing here. The doctors, priests, shopkeepers, and mechanics are German, Greeks, Armenians, and Jews. . . . Prince Stirbey, the Hospodar of Wallachia, has been deposed, according to the last accounts,

I

from Bucharest. He is a great favourer of the
Austrians. The latter want to hold the principalities during the winter, which they will do, if
we have not finished our work before it commences.
They are very much opposed to the union. Ghika,
the Moldavian Hospodar, is for the union. I was
introduced to him when I was at Jassy, as I think
I told you before. Russian and Moldavian are the
only languages spoken by the peasants; and of
French and German, the latter is the more useful.

P.S.—I am learning a little Russian. Чарлесъ
Гордонъ is Charles Gordon in Russian.

Akermann, Aug. 23, 1856.—We are still here,
haggling about the frontier, but shall not remain
much longer over it. I hope to get away to the
tracing out on the ground itself in about ten days'
time. We have got a troublesome Moldave prince
named Stourdza, who is the second commissioner
for Turkey. He is always sparring with the
Russians, and delaying the work. The weather
here is very pleasant, not too hot; and, as far as we
have gone yet, the climate is not unhealthy. The
papers are full of the Kars heroes, but they think
here that too little notice has been taken of the
Hungarians who were in that place. Mouravief is
thought a great muff by the majority of the Russian

officers who know him. The foreigners laugh at the way we *féte* and the deal we talk. Stokes,* a major of Royal Engineers, is appointed on the commission for the better navigation of the Danube—a very difficult question, and one that will take a long time to settle. The entrance of the Dniester is closed by a narrow spit of land, which has two openings, one being one-sixth of a mile, the other three-quarters of a mile. The latter is only four or five feet deep; the former, seven or eight feet deep. None of our vessels entered the Dniester. It is a great pity that such an important river should be so narrow. We are now engaged in making plans of the frontier to be sent to our Government, and it is very troublesome work.

Galatz, Sept. 29, 1856.—It is a long time since I wrote, or since I have heard from you; and although I have very little to tell you, I shall break the silence. I have come here for a couple of days from Bolgrad, where I am at present located, and am engaged on the plans of the frontier, which are thirty-two in number. The commission has gone on to Seratzika, after which we shall all return to Reni, where we remain until everything is finished,

* Now Colonel Sir John Stokes, R.E.

as the Russians refuse to quit Russia. No settlement
has been yet made about Bolgrad. The French
Government have given up the point to the
Russians; but our Government, with the Turks
and Austrians, hold out for Bolgrad being transferred
to the Moldavians. It will be a great triumph over
the Russians if we carry it against them and the
French. I expect there is a hot paper warfare
going on at present between our Governments about
it. Colonel Besson has presented Stanton and me
with small likenesses of himself. I do not admire
the small ones, whatever the large ones may be like.
I will send you a view of Bolgrad, etc., in my next,
and would send some game, but it is rather far.
Major Stokes is here; he is a commissioner for the
Danube. The climate is delightful in Bessarabia.
It is only those people who live badly and eat
enormously of melons and other similar things who
get ill. It is a tremendous country for melons,
gourds, pumpkins, etc., of every colour, shape, and
size. The grape harvest has commenced—not many
this year. It is all the same, I think, for their wine
is nothing but bad vinegar. The corn crops are not
so productive. We get *caviare* here moderately
cheap. Galatz has not come up to what the State
people expected it would on the opening of the

Danube. Odessa has taken most of the trade in bringing articles which the Russians were deprived of during the war. I can hear nothing of their doings in Sebastopol.

Kichenief, Nov. 10, 1856.—I just write a line to tell the result of a wolf excursion which we undertook the other day. We got together about 200 peasants, and about fifty guns, viz. Stanton, James, myself, Prince Stourdza, the second Turkish commissioner, Colonel Besson, some eight or ten Russian employés, and the remainder peasants. The forest was about twenty-five miles from Kichenief, so we slept at a village the night before, and next day surrounded a portion of the forest and commenced operations. I did not get a shot the first day ; and our bag altogether was five foxes, twenty-eight hares, no wolves. The following day we went to another forest and surrounded a place where the peasants had seen some wolves the night before. We, the shooters, were usually placed not more than twenty-eight yards apart, so as to render it impossible for a wolf to escape. We, however, once neglected this precaution, and through it lost seven wolves, as there were nine in the forest and only two were killed. Four foxes and twenty-five hares

completed the bag. I got four shots, and killed
two hares; Stanton killed a fox the day before,
and one hare this day. It is not bad fun, but
rather butchery, as the hares, wolves, etc., try and
break the line and run the gauntlet of all the
guns until killed. I had a shot at a wolf and
hit him, but he got off. I had small shot, No. 4,
and he was in the bush. We had greyhounds on
the outskirts of the forest, who coursed the hares
that escaped from the shooters. The wolves are
bigger than dogs, and have larger jaws. They are
very formidable in winter, and attack men; as yet
it is too early for them to do this. There are also
small deer here, but we did not see any on this
occasion. I wish you were with us for the shooting. . . . I have killed about 100 head of game
of different sorts this year, and will send you a
description of our next hunt. I am afraid I shall
not be home until April, as there does not seem any
sign of the question of Bolgrad being settled. The
Russian commissioners are trying to get the French
Government to change their commissioner, as they
do not like the way he treats them. The Russians
here rob us right and left.

Kichenief, Nov. 10, 1856.—The Russians are the

people who cut the letters, and do everything to annoy the writers of letters. Their prices are absurdly high, and each letter receives a receipt from the post-office. The winter has set in here very sharp. We had a quantity of snow on the 6th, and severe frost ever since. We went on a wolf excursion * the other day, and slept at a village twenty-five versts from here. The French colonel, and Prince Stourdza, the second Turkish commissioner, went with us, and some Russian employés. There are some small deer not very far from here. Our plans go on rather slowly, and we shall be at this place until March or April, I think, and then probably there will be some difficulty, as the Russians will delay giving up the territory as long as possible. You cannot conceive the way in which the Russian merchants pillage us, and, in addition to that, their articles are so bad as to break and come to pieces on using them. I detest the merchants of Russia whom I have seen here, and I do not know any good thing about them. They make a joke of pillaging the commissioners. I have not heard any corps news for a long time. What is about to take place in the corps ? How are the Woolwich authorities getting on ? Send me out *Jackson's Journal* if you can.

* Described in previous letter to a different correspondent.

Kichenief, Nov. 18, 1856.—We are now in the
midst of snow and frost, snow having commenced
on November 6, which is very early for these
parts. It is at present about eight inches deep.
If you can manage it, and my father can spare it,
I should like the plan, on thin paper, of the Sebastopol lines to be sent out to me. I will endeavour
to get him another on my return. The Russians
are still antipathetic towards the commission, and
(although I should not go if there was any society)
no one has thought of asking the commissioners to
dinner, not even the governor of Bessarabia. The
commissioners went to one public dinner, and that
has been all. The Governor-General of Bessarabia
asked Colonel Besson, the French commissioner, to
tea, and they played whist afterwards, and he had
to pay 6*s.* 8*d.* to the governor for the use of packs
of cards! We are assured that 36,000 roubles have
been given by the Russian Government to enter-
tain us and lodge us well, but the officials put it all
in their own pockets instead. I do not say this
because I should like their acquaintance, but to
give you a notion of their perquisites. There are
about 2000 soldiers here, but we never see them;
they are quartered on the inhabitants, as all the
Russian soldiers are.

There is a chance of the commission being broken up, as the Governments cannot agree about Bolgrad, and I should not be surprised if the Russians refused to cede anything. The French Government is at the bottom of all this. We have begun sledging here, but it is rather early; and sometimes when the peasants come in on sledges, they find the snow thawed before they return, and have to go back in mud. I should think you have had a great deal of work lately, and am very glad to hear that you are well with all the worry. The Danube commission has commenced its labour at last, when the Danube will be frozen in a month. Major Stokes has his family at Galatz. Stanton makes a capital commissioner, and is very much liked by the others. Colonel Besson, the French commissioner, lives with us; he is very lively, and preferable to the generality of Frenchmen. He does not like the Russians a bit better than we do, in spite of his Government. I think we have got a very good Secretary of State for Foreign Affairs in Lord Clarendon, as his despatches and instructions are extremely clear and straightforward. I will try and send you a newspaper which has undergone the ordeal of the Russian censor, who blacks out all matter that is displeasing to the

Government. The letters are only pricked to annoy people, as there is no quarantine at present.

Kichenief, Dec. 6, 1856.—We are in the middle of winter—snow, etc. Thermometer 7°, and they say that it will last like this for two months longer. The plans are getting on, although there are a good many still to do. We are now in a very comfortable house, and have it all to ourselves. It belongs to a Russian colonel, who is at Moscow. Mr. Russell, the *Times* correspondent, and a namesake of ours, a Mr. Lewis Gordon, called here on their way to England from the Crimea. Mr. Russell had travelled overland from Moscow, taking thirteen days to Sebastopol. Sebastopol, he says, is just as it was left. Nothing has yet been done, and it will remain untouched for two years. The American engineers in the Russian service hoped to be able to get the sunken vessels (seventy-seven in number) up again. Mr. Russell had an interpreter with him, who served in our commissariat service in the Crimea. He wished us to take him, but luckily we did not; for we got a note from Mr. Russell, dated Chernovitz, on the Austrian frontier, in which he warns us against the said interpreter, who had absconded, and taken away a sheep-skin coat, boots, and the drag-chain of Russell's carriage. The Russians are still cool, and are rather annoyed at the rumour of the cession of Bolgrad. If this rumour is true we shall finish by March, and I may be home by April. What is going on at Woolwich?—any squabbles? I hope you are all well, and will have a happy Christmas. . . . I have some plans, beautiful prints, with the Russian idea of the principal events of the war, for you. They have most absurd ideas on the subject, as you will see.

Kichenief, Dec. 29, 1856.—The posts are infamous in Russia. Your letter took nine days coming from Jassy. We are all quite well, and I have got over the whole of my work, until the questions are settled, which I believe will be very soon, as the Russians themselves say that Bolgrad will be given up to Moldavia, and that will be a great crow for us. If we hear soon, and commence the work at once, it will take us (to complete the whole thing) up to the middle of March, 1857. Colonel Besson has gone to Jassy, and Dervish Pasha to Constantinople, for a month or so. The latter talks English very well, and appears a very good specimen of his class. Fanton, the Russian commissioner, is a very wily old chap, and full of lawyers' tricks; he is a Frenchman by birth, but naturalized in his new country. Kichenief is the last place I should like to remain in ; it is so dreadfully dull. The governors of the districts were warned a few weeks ago to prepare for war, which I think was much nearer than people thought ; however, I suppose it will be all settled now. One of the Turkish officers, a young fellow, died of consumption at Jassy the other day. He was attached to the commission, and had been ill for some time. The Russian officers are very much put out at Bolgrad being given up, and say they cannot understand it. Articles of food are very cheap here, meat being about twopence a pound ; on the other hand, groceries are exorbitantly dear. . . . The Russians have twenty-five war steamers in the Caspian sea, and are augmenting their troops in that quarter.

P.S.—*Jan.* 1, 1857.—Many happy returns of the day to all.

Kichenief, Jan. 9, 1857.—We are now settled as to the frontier questions. Russia has given up Bolgrad and received a portion of territory in exchange equal to that surrendered, both as to number of inhabitants and also as to extent of land. This mode of compensation will give us more than half our work to do over again. I had almost finished my plans, and one-half of these will have to be re-drawn. However, it is a consolation to know that the thing is settled. We heard all this by telegraph from Paris, and by the same message learnt that we were to proceed at once to work on the frontier, in order to get it finished by March 30, and thus allow of the ceded territory being handed over to the Moldavians on that day. We start in a few days, although the thermometer is down to 4°. You may imagine what a hurry they are in to get this finished. The Russians pretend to believe that they have got the best of the dispute, but it will be difficult to persuade the world to be of the same opinion. Although so cold, there is not much snow, and it is beautifully clear weather, capital for sledging. Dervish Pasha, who left for Constantinople, will not return, I think, although he is the first Turkish commissioner. The new frontier leaves Tobak and Bolgrad in Moldavia, and gives a piece of land near the Pruth in exchange to Russia. The Russian commissioner had a finger in that Russian document which you probably saw in the newspapers, and which is full of misstatements. We are going to have our carriages put on skates for our voyage, but take the wheels with us in case of a thaw. The Austrians are rectifying their

frontier with Moldavia, and are taking large tracts
of the latter country into their possession.   Some
people have gone to bed Moldavian, and awoke
Austrian—never the contrary.   I believe that the
consuls have protested, and that there will be a
fuss about it.

Kichenief, Jan. 12, 1857.—I thought that my previous letter would have been the last before we left
for the frontier, but the day I sent it off I received
the map of Sebastopol quite safe, and not hurt in
the least.   I do not understand the value you seem
to place on plans of this sort; when once the plate is
made it is only the paper that costs anything; and
why there should be anything difficult in any one,
wishing to get these plans and able to pay for them,
obtaining them is beyond my comprehension.   If
the plans were of forts in our possession, it would
be another affair.   I have sent home to our office
numerous plans, and I suppose no one has seen them
except a chosen few.   When I come home I will
try and root them out.   You may not know, perhaps,
that the plan of the battle of Alma was found,
accidentally, hidden away in an old drawer.   I shall
endeavour to obtain the complete set of Sebastopol
photographs, on my way home, and also a few

extra ones taken by a French photographer, whom I met on board the Austrian Lloyd steamer. I have also got some capital prints of the war, very well prepared, and with excellent likenesses of some of the principal Russian generals; of these I have altogether fifty-six. Now that we have put on skates to our carriages, it has begun to thaw very rapidly, and the mud is axletree deep in the streets. To-day is the Russian New Year, and people are calling on each other. As for music, I do not think it is to be had, for I do not believe that the Russians have more than two tunes which can be called really Russian. James's grandfather, Sir R. Gardner, is dead; we heard this last week. We start in a week. The courier with the map signed by the Paris congress, has not yet arrived. I enclose a tracing of the signatures of our commission; they are placed in the alphabetical order of the countries represented, but the signature of the Commissary who owns the place comes first of all. The population of the ceded territory is 154,000. I am interested in the staff of the army, and would like to know if we are eligible for entrance.

Kichenief, Jan. 29, 1857.—We expect to be away from this place for three weeks or a month,

when we return here to finish our plans, etc. We
have made the acquaintance of some very nice
people here, who are excessively kind. They are
Moldavians, but own property in Bessarabia.
The territory will be given over in two parts. The
southern consists of Ismail, Kilia, Peni, and
Bolgrad, as well as the delta of the Danube. The
northern part consists of the land between the
Pruth and the Yalpukh. The French colonel has
been obliged to send his servant back to France
viâ Odessa. The winter seems to be over, but the
roads are as bad as in the Crimea during the worst
time, and the low lands are flooded from the melting
of the snow. The Danube has not, up to the present, been frozen this year, which is an extraordinary
occurrence. Do you notice that Mr. Russell has
commenced writing his adventures? We received
our instructions about the change of frontier before
any of the others except the Russians, which
shows our Government to be very prompt. The
others have not yet received theirs. There are lots
of princesses here and princes, as all the children
of a prince have the same title, so you may
imagine how they increase. Their coats of arms
are very peculiar. I enclose one for your inspec-
tion. It is like a trophy of arms.

Bolgrad, Feb. 9, 1857.—I have only a little time to write, and not very much to tell you beyond the intelligence that we have finished the frontier as far as this place, and expect to have done the whole in less than a week. We left Kichenief on Saturday, January 31, and came down to Doljeler, a village on the frontier, by a road passing through the Prussian colonies, which are superior to any other in Bessarabia. They do not pay any duties or taxes, beyond a capitation tax of eightpence per annum. All these colonies were established in 1813, and the villages are called after the battles gained in the Leipzig campaign. The weather yesterday was most terribly cold ; the thermometer must have been below zero. The cold was more intense than I ever felt before. A breeze accompanied it, and it was as much as we could do to take the angles with the theodolite. Bottles of sherry wrapped in straw were frozen. The day before was not agreeable, what with snow and wind. The snow, luckily, is not very deep. To-day is not so bad, as the wind has fallen. Before this reaches you the southern part of Bessarabia and the delta of the Danube will be given over to Moldavia, and in a fortnight all the land will be ceded. We return to Kichenief, and when all the

K

plans are done—in about six weeks, I suppose—our work will be over. I have not heard whether the Danube is frozen, but should think that it is as Lake Yalpukh is, although the ice is not very thick.

Kichenief, Feb. 19, 1857.—We have at last arrived at the end of the actual marking out of the frontier, and are very glad of it, for the villages were very unpleasant places to live in. We returned here on the 15th, and have commenced our plans, which we may hope to complete entirely by the end of March. The territory will be handed over on March 8, and a commission of Moldaves will arrive shortly to take it over. The weather is beautiful now, just like the Crimea. Count Strogonoff, the governor-general, is expected here daily to arrange the posts, etc. The new territory adds a quarter to the revenue of Moldavia, which is something. We have not much news here. There are a good many parties, etc., as usual before Lent. I have not received the Jacksons' list. I received your last letter, dated January 16 or 19, on February 12, which is a quick arrival; but to make up for that I received, on the 17th, a letter dated October 16, 1856. My letters generally take ten days going from here to Jassy.

We have here at present the general who commands all the posts of Russia, and who is endeavouring to put things right in this quarter. Only a general officer is eligible for this employment.

Kichenief, March 5, 1857.—We are rather dull now, as the Careme or Lent has begun; but we are still very much occupied during the day, and expect to be six weeks before we finish. Count Strogonoff, the governor-general of Little Russia, is here concerning the cession of the territory. It would have been given over some time before, if the Moldaves had been ready, but they are dreadful people for any business. I have just heard from Jassy that the Caimacan Balsch is dead. He died of chest complaint. There will be tremendous intriguing about his successor, as it will have great weight on the union question. It is beautiful weather, and quite light until half-past six o'clock. Most of the people here are fasting. There is a grand ceremony in the cathedral on Sunday, during which all nations not of the Orthodox Church (Greek) are cursed. The Russians are rather ashamed of the ceremony, and it is to take place early to prevent strangers attending.

Kichenief, March 30, 1857.—I am afraid that it
is some time since I wrote, but I will explain the
reason. About a fortnight ago Stanton received
a telegraphic despatch from Lord Clarendon, order-
ing him to hand over the officers and men now
with him to Colonel Simmons * for the Asiatic
boundary. I did not care much about going, and
telegraphed to ask if any exchange would be per-
mitted. To-day I have received an answer to say
that I must go. I had waited for this reply to
let you know for certain. We shall probably leave
this in ten days, as the plans, etc., are at last
finished. I leave for Galatz and Constantinople
with James and the men. We shall meet Simmons
at the latter place. We know nothing about the
Asian frontier, but believe it is not of great
extent. The frontier has been already marked out,
but there is a little dispute about the locality of a
river Araxes. The Mount Ararat is quite close to
the frontier. We do not know how long it will
take, but I will let you know as soon as I do. I
shall send home some things to you by Stanton,
and also give directions for my trunk (which has
turned up at last) to be sent to you. I have done
some plans for General Jones, which perhaps I will

* The present Sir Lintorn Simmons, Governor of Gibraltar.

ask you to forward to him at Sandhurst. We are very dull here, and the weather is again very bad. However, we have been so much employed that we have scarcely been out for ten days. I hope Lord Palmerston will remain in office. You have no idea what interest foreigners take in our debates. I will write once more from this place, and then from Galatz and Constantinople.

Kichenief, April 10, 1857.—You will have received my last letter telling you that I am ordered to join Colonel Simmons for the boundary in Asia. We leave this in two days, and I will write from Galatz, where we take the Austrian steamer for Constantinople. We have finished our work, everything has been signed, and the total number of the plans we have made is upwards of 100. For my part, I have had enough of them for my whole life. I hope you will not follow ——'s advice about moving to London. I do not see the advantage to be gained by going from the country into a smoky town. Every one here is preparing to start. The Russian commissioners are very angry at our going away so quickly, as they themselves will be forced to go to St. Petersburg during a time that the roads are in the most dreadful condition.   Stanton goes home direct with his plans, etc., and will arrive soon after this letter. The people here are quite excited about Lord Palmerston; they hope he will not succeed in the appeal to the country.   I hope he will.*

Galatz, April 16, 1857.—Only a few lines to let you know that I have arrived here safely, and leave for Constantinople in a day or so.   Stanton and myself went through Jassy, and came down to this by the banks of the Sereth, which are beautifully wooded.   We had the Carpathians in view most of the way, and had splendid weather, although it is scarcely late enough for the trees to be green.   A wolf crossed over the road in broad daylight, not ten yards from our horses; they are very bold in this country, but they rarely go as far as this.   The newly ceded territory is in great disorder.   The inhabitants refuse to obey the Moldaves, and own nobody's authority.   This is caused, I suspect, by Russian intrigues.   It is just eleven months since we arrived here for the Bessarabian Commission, and now we are let in

---

* This is referring to Lord Palmerston's celebrated appeal to the country on the China question.   It may be added that the country enthusiastically responded, and supported the Minister against the House of Commons.

for another. I will send a box of things home from Constantinople. Let me know anything you may want, as I would much rather send them than choose myself useless things.

In a letter to a friend, dated Galatz, April 15, 1857, General Gordon describes the same events in slightly different language : "We are on our travels again, and I am sorry to say not homeward bound. We left Kichenief for this place three days ago, and Stanton and I have just arrived from Jassy, having had a splendid journey through the valley of the Sereth river to this place, the Carpathian mountains in view most of the way. The country is beautifully wooded, and we went along capitally, posting with six horses, and doing ten and eleven miles an hour. Stanton goes straight home through Vienna, and I, unfortunately, am let in for Simmons's commission, which I do not at all admire. However, G—— was as inflexible as usual. I tried him with a telegraphic message, and received an answer in four words that 'Lieutenant Gordon must go.' Thanks for your letter, which I should have answered before, but towards the end I was so hard worked. I had to do a plan for the French colonel as well as our own. The commission for the principalities is commencing its work, and it will be very difficult, for the Moldaves are the most fickle and intriguing people on the earth. They ape the French in everything, and are full of ceremony, dress, etc. Stokes is here, but what the Danube Commission is about no one knows. I think the principality question is likely to produce some violent effects in Europe. The employés sent by the Moldavian Government to take over the ceded territory have been receiving bribes and trafficking in a most disgraceful manner. The consequence is that the new territory is in a state of anarchy, and, probably through Russian intrigues, the people have cast off all authority."

Constantinople, April 23, 1857.—We arrived from Galatz on the 21st, after a very good voyage. We found Simmons here with his secretary, and I believe we are all to meet in Erzeroum on May 15. The frontier proves to be very long, twice the length of the Bessarabian frontier, and I believe it will be nearly two years before we finish it, as it has to be fixed much more in detail than the other. I have got some photographs to send you, and shall endeavour to do so by private hand if possible. I will tell you more about that in my next letter.

Constantinople is quite empty; nothing like what it was during the war. I am sorry I cannot give you any more particulars about our future work, but it is not, apparently, determined what the frontier is to be. I am very much disappointed in not seeing you all, but I might be able to get away from the commission in the winter, when no work can be done. I had an interview with Lord Stratford to-day to give over the plans of the frontier. He was very kind, and questioned me about the frontier. He wished that we had held out for the whole of Bessarabia, when it would have been worth having. I dined with him in the evening, and Lady Stratford is a very nice person. We leave this next week for Trebizonde; it will take three days to get there by steamer. I will write you a daily journal of our doings.

Constantinople, April 27, 1857.—We leave this the day after to-morrow. I shall keep all the prints I have until I return, but send you a few photographs of Sebastopol, etc., which you have not got.

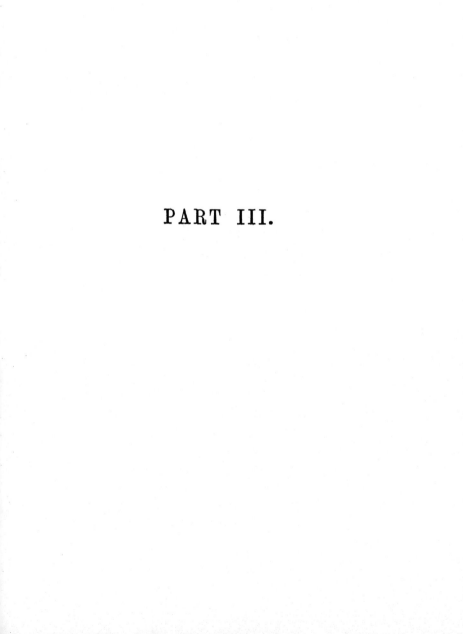

PART III.

LETTERS FROM ARMENIA.

———◆◆◆———

Trebizonde, May 7, 1857.—We left Constantinople on May 1, on board the Turkish steamer
Kars. It was in a beastly state of dirt, the deck
being crowded with Turks and Armenians returning
from different pilgrimages, some from Mecca and
others from Jerusalem. We coasted along close to
the land, which is very mountainous, and arrived the
next day at Sinope. The Turks have broken up
the ships which were sunk by the Russians, and
recovered some of the guns. There is an old castle
at Sinope which was built by the Genoese, and it is
in the most perfect preservation, the masonry being
equal to that of the present day. We stopped
about three hours there, and went about the place.
We had very smooth water, which was a fortunate
thing for the mass of people on deck. The mountains
all along are very much higher than any I have

ever seen, and are very much broken. Trebizonde is a very pretty town; it has a great many ruins about it, and is infinitely cleaner than Constantinople. Our caravan alone consists of eighty horses, and will cost about £230 for the journey between this and Erzeroum. The French commissioner, Colonel Pelissier, has only four people with him, and he has about ten horses. We have three interpreters, three cooks, and innumerable servants of every description. We leave this to-morrow, and take ten days going to Erzeroum, a distance of only 180 miles, but extremely mountainous. We pass a range to-morrow about 10,000 feet above the sea. You shall have a description of our further journey. At present I have not much to tell you, as we are busy packing up our things, and getting our immense party organized. We have a medical man with us. I have not heard from you for a long time, but I believe that we shall receive the mail to-day.

Erzeroum, May 25, 1857.—We left Trebizonde on May 13, with a caravan of ninety-nine horses, all in our service, and arrived here on the 22nd. The road is very bad in some places, and one can scarcely go further than twenty miles per diem, any pace quicker than a walk being quite impossible. No such thing as a wheeled carriage is to be seen. Every evening we encamped, and started early the next day. The country is exceedingly mountainous. We passed two ranges of mountains 9000 to 10,000 feet high. We had frost and snow during our journey, and a good deal of rain, which made camping out anything but agreeable. The inhabitants are very poor, and in their primitive condition. They sleep in houses which serve as stables and dwelling-places at the same time, there being only a simple partition between the cattle and the inhabitants. Everything is very dear. Forage costs as much as in England. This is a serious drawback in a country where horses are the only mode of moving about. All the trade of Asia Minor comes by this road, but it is hampered by the cost of transport, as you may judge from our caravan here having cost £404. The French commissioner has not yet arrived. He is not fit for this work, being quite fatigued with his first day's journey, and obliged to stay at a village on the way. The Turkish commissioner could get no money from the Government for his journey. He was directed to take any horses he could lay his hands on; the consequence being that he stopped on the road caravans on their way to Constantinople from Persia, threw off their goods, put his own on the animals, and made them carry them. This is not so much the fault of the commissioner, as of the Government, which would not give him money.

Erzeroum is a very pretty place at a distance, but horribly dirty when entered; it is situated in a large valley, and the Euphrates, which is a very small stream here, runs through it. The mountains around are still covered with snow. There is no spring, but twenty or thirty days of summer, after which two or two and a half months of autumn, and then eight or nine months of very hard winter. The town is 7000 or 8000 feet above the sea. The people are a collection of Armenians, Turks, and Persians. I do not see any Jews, although the Armenians resemble them rather in their appearance, and certainly in their dealings. We have a very good surgeon with us, and we are pretty comfortable as yet. I like Simmons, who is very well read, and amusing. We leave this for Kars in three or four days, and from there we go to meet the Russian commissioner at Gumri. As far as the frontier is concerned we do not know anything more. I shall write again from Kars, which, from all accounts, is in a deplorable state. Horses are very dear here on account of the war. I have got another, having sold my Crimean one to an officer of Cossacks in Bessarabia. The prints are coming home to you; I could not send them by Stanton, as he went overland, and every package adds to the expense of travelling. Your letters will be at least six weeks or two months coming here, or perhaps more, on account of the numerous changes of hands.

P.S.—We left a barometer at Trebizonde for observation at that place. A fire occurred in the town after we left, and the house in which the barometer had been put caught fire. It was fortunately rescued from the flames, when the nails holding it to the wall were red hot, and the mercury had risen almost to bursting point. It would have been a great nuisance had it been destroyed, as our observations taken here depend upon it.

Kars, June 17, 1857.—I received your last kind letter at Erzeroum just before we left for this place, and with it Curzon's Armenia, for which I am very much obliged. We have been here eight days surveying the place, Simmons having gone on to Gumri, on the frontier, to meet the Russian com-

L

missioner. We are to rejoin him the day after to-morrow. The road between this town and Erze-roum is very much better than that between the latter place and Trebizonde. Kars is, as you can easily imagine, a ruined city, and may, perhaps, never recover its former strength and importance. As far as the works of defence are concerned they are excessively badly traced. A little pamphlet published by Kmety, a Hungarian, gives a graphic description of the siege. One thing difficult if not impossible to realize, without seeing it, is the large extent of the position. We are in summer at last, 85° in the shade; but there is generally a breeze in the plain, so that it is not very oppres-sive. Until we get to Gumri I can tell you no-thing about how long our labours are likely to last, but as soon as I arrive there I will let you know. I think it very probable that I may obtain leave during the winter. Kars has been twice in the hands of the Russians during the last thirty years, Paskievitch having taken it by assault in 1829. I am very busy at present with this survey, but we shall probably finish it to-morrow. We are up a good height here; the barometer stands at 24°, and sometimes less, and the hills around are partially covered with now. Mount Alagos, the rival of Mount Ararat, is in view of our camp, and I believe Mount Ararat can be seen at certain times. Our feeding is pretty good, but the drinking is not. I believe, however, that it will improve as soon as we reach the frontier. Pelissier, the French commissioner, travels in a cage, which is supported between two mules. He is much too old to be sent on an expedition like this. He had, as you know, already been laid up between Trebizonde and Erzeroum. I have to get up my mathematics again, for we are required to make observations for latitude and longitude, and this takes up a good deal of my time. I am getting more expert now than at first with my star-gazing.

P.S.—Kmety's pamphlet is entitled " A Narrative of the Defence of Kars."

Gumri, or Alexandropol, June 21, 1857.—You had a very dull letter in my last, and I will endeavour to give you a better one this time. We left Kars with the intention of measuring and surveying the road between it and Gumri. This part of the country is not nearly as mountainous as that we passed through in our former journeys. But it presented another very sad and striking feature in the number of perfectly deserted villages, which the inhabitants had left as long ago as Paskievitch's first invasion of the country in 1829. He then persuaded upwards of 60,000 of the inhabitants to emigrate to Russian territory, and the gap left by this exodus has never been filled up. These villages dot the country in all directions, and they each of them have a square tower with loopholes intended for the protection of their families against any sudden inroad of the Kurds or other wandering tribes, who might wish to carry them off into slavery. We saw Ararat for the first time on June 18. It is a very fine mountain, rising alone in the plain, and covered with snow, at least it is so at the present moment. Mount Alagos, its rival, is also in view, but has not the same fine appearance as Ararat. The same day we passed the battle-field of Kuyukdere, where the Russians, in very small force under Bebutoff, were attacked by a very superior force of Turks under the direction of General Guyon, the Hungarian.* By some mistake the Turkish left lost

* General Count Guyon was one of the few adventurous soldiers of fortune which the present century has given us. In that character he seemed to be almost a survival of the last century. An Englishman by birth, and the son of an officer in our service, his family had been long established in the West of England. At an early age he entered the Austrian army, as a cadet in a regi-

its way during the night, and was eight miles
distant from the field when the right came into
action. The battle was very hotly contested; but
the Turks had at last to retire, with the loss of
several guns. Had the affair gone off as Guyon
intended, the Russians would have been licked.
This battle, I should add, was fought in August,
1854, and before any English officer had arrived in
this country. The Russian loss was very severe;
there were 3200 wounded alone brought into Gumri
for treatment.

ment of Hungarian cavalry. On the outbreak of the Hungarian
rebellion Guyon was entrusted with a command, and obtained
some successes. He refused to accept the terms offered by the
Austrian Government, and fled to Turkey, where he joined the
Sultan's service. Shortly before the outbreak of hostilities with
Russia, he proceeded to Armenia in high military command, and
it is to the incidents of the early campaign on the Asiatic frontier
that General Gordon refers above. After the war General Guyon
was made Pasha of Damascus, where some years later he died
suddenly, and not without a suspicion of having been poisoned.
The manner in which he obtained the title of Count exhibits the
habit of an age that is passing away. When a young man he
obtained and reciprocated the affection of a member of one of the
proudest and noblest Hungarian families. At that time he had
no title, and his offer of marriage was haughtily rejected. Determined not to be beaten, he spent his military leave in a journey to
Sardinia, where he purchased the necessary title, and returning as
Count Guyon de Geyse he was accepted as the suitor of the lady
of his choice. Guyon was a man of great personal strength and
high courage.

On our first arrival here we met a Polish doctor who has been exiled for ten years, of which only four had passed away, and he told us that the Russian loss from sickness during the late war was enormous. Upwards of 700 men died every month at Gumri during the blockade of Kars. This statement does not take into any account those who died before Kars itself, or on the road from thirst and other causes. If one-tenth part of the mismanagement of this Russian army had happened to us, it would have been infinitely worse than our Crimean misery.

There is a pretty strong fortress here, but there are not many troops, most of them being employed in the Caucasus itself. Mount Alagos is an extinct volcano, but before becoming so it emitted a tremendous flow of lava, and inundated the whole of this valley. This lava bed is ten feet deep, and underneath it there is any amount of alluvial soil. The lava is perfectly level, and has about two feet of earth over it. The Russians have cut the ditches for their fortress in this lava bed, and the sides stand up quite perpendicularly.

The frontier commission have, I think, four points in dispute, but all of minor consideration ; and it is, therefore, probable that we shall be able to finish

our work during the present year, which I shall
be very glad of, as this commission is no benefit
to me in the way of either honour or money. We,
that is, James and myself, are to be each detached
with one officer of the Russian etat-major, and one
Turkish, to verify the plans of the frontier; firstly,
towards Mount Ararat, and then towards the north.
We start on Tuesday next. You shall hear from
me on our road. I do not think it would be
interesting to you to learn about my daily proceedings, for there is a great sameness about them; and
when we are encamped in tents you can imagine
that it is very uncomfortable to write. General
Tchirikoff is a very polite, gentlemanly Russian;
but as deep as a well. He keeps up much greater
state than did the general who was with us in
Bessarabia, who, I hear by the way, has since got
a very good post at Warsaw. The Turks, as usual,
are quite behind every one else in their business
arrangements. An instance of this is the following. A chronometer was sent here from Constantinople. It arrived at Kars in three days
from Trebizonde, having travelled the whole way
at a gallop. When it arrived it had lost one hour;
but the funniest thing about it was that it was
accompanied by a letter particularly requesting

that it should not be put upon a horse. They say here that the whole Russian army in the Caucasus dies out in seven years.* Its strength is 150,000 men. This mortality is not so much from the climate as from bad feeding. I have never been in better health than at present. We have got a very large staff with us, which is rather un-necessary, as the Russians have done nearly all the work beforehand.

P.S.—I enclose the signatures of the commission : Pellissier, French ; Simmons, English ; Tchirikoff and Ivanin, Russian ; Hussein Pasha and Osman Bey, Turkish.

* In a later letter, that of September 28, the writer states, on presumably better data, that it died out in five years.

THE FORTRESS OF ALEXANDROPOL.

The fortress of Alexandropol (40° 47′ N. lat. 43° 45′ E. long., 4500 feet above the sea) is situated on the left bank of the river Arpatchai, which here forms the boundary between Russia and Turkey. It is distant thirty-five miles from Kars, and eighty-four miles from Tiflis. The plain on which it is situated is perfectly level, and very peculiar. It has a stratum of alluvial soil for the depth of one foot six inches on the surface, and then a substratum of fine uniform lava ten to fifteen feet thick, supposed to have issued from Mount Alagos (13,450 feet), an extinct volcano thirty miles from Alexandropol. The depth of the earth allows the growth of grain, but entirely prevents that of trees, which with their roots cannot penetrate into the lava. The Russians have taken advantage of this bed of lava in the ditch of the fortress.

The fortress is well constructed, and in perfect repair. There are upwards of 200 guns (varying from 36-prs. to 12-prs.) mounted on the works, and about 100 in reserve, of which thirty are field guns with their equipment, waggons, etc. The garrison would be 5000 to 6000, including artillery. There are large supplies of ammunition and military stores. The ditch, twelve feet deep, of the two western fronts has not been excavated near the flanks, on account of the expense. The Russians have constructed in the centres of the two curtains a *caponnière* with two guns in each flank to defend the dead angles caused by the non-excavation of the whole of the ditch. In the centre of these two fronts is a large *caponnière* mounting ten guns in the upper tier and eight in the lower tier. This *caponnière* is on a lower level than the *enceinte* of the place. The counterscarp at the north-west and south-west angles of these two fronts is for the distance of twenty yards composed of a crenellated wall four feet six inches thick. This was caused by the irregularity of the ground. The bomb-proof barracks of the northern fronts mount in casemate two tiers of fourteen guns at the curtains. The flanks have five guns in casemates open to the rear, in addition to the guns on the parapet above. The lunette in the ditch is eight feet deep. The eastern front has an escarp fourteen feet high cut in the lava, and well flanked by the *caponnière* defending the entrances mounting four guns.

The bomb-proof barracks in the southern fronts have one tier of eight guns in casemate at the curtains, and three guns in each flank in casemates open to the rear.

The two outworks are closed at the gorge with a loopholed wall, flanked by a small guard house. They have no ditches, but. an escarp of ten feet in the lava.

The tower (marked A in my plan) is sixty yards in diameter, with a well in the centre. It has its gorge closed with a ditch and loopholed wall. It mounts fifteen guns on the top and fifteen guns in casemate. It is proposed to connect it by a crenellated wall to the main work. The tower (marked B) has a ditch and small glacis. It mounts eight guns in casemate and eight guns on the top. Its object is to flank the long ravine which runs southward from it.

All the buildings in the interior of the fortress are bomb-proof. The great fault of the fortress, as it is constructed at present, is that it does not so much as see the town, with its population of 9310. It is now proposed, however, to make a large work on the site (marked K) with the view of meeting this want.

During the war in 1853, when the Turks were 35,000 strong at Baiandour, six miles from Alexandropol, and the Russians had only two battalions in the fortress, the latter demolished all the houses which were on this ground.

I think that, should it ever be in our power to besiege this place (which is not likely from the enormous difficulty of getting a siege train there), that batteries might be established on the hillocks between the fortress and the river to breach the large *caponniere* and the tower A, which, from the formation of the ground, would not be opposed by more fire than the direct fire of the works they were intended to breach, and which would be limited by their circular form to about seven guns. The soil is not unfavourable on these hills.

The hill on which the cemetery of the officers killed at Kars and Kuyukdere is situated is also favourable for batteries.

The principal well, which is sunk to a good depth, is in the north-eastern bastion.

Hadji Birami, July 2, 1857.—I have been here three days, having finished my examination of the frontier for sixty versts in five days in extremely

hot weather. The first day from Gumri* we passed
Baiandoor, where the Turks and Russians had a
small battle in 1853, and where the former lost a
splendid opportunity of taking Gumri, which was
nearly denuded of troops. My Turkish colleague,
who is delegated to verify the frontier with me,
was present, and got into Gumri as a spy disguised
in the character of a servant. The Russian army
avenged the slight check they received from the
Turks by taking all their artillery of the right
wing soon after, and with this affair the campaign
of 1853 ended.

At the place from which I am writing there are
seltzer water springs, which I took care not to
drink. My Russian colleague is a very good fellow
as far as I can make out, not being able to speak to
him. The third day of our tour we passed through
Ani † the ancient capital of Armenia. This city is
completely deserted, and has splendid churches
still standing in it. These churches are capitally
built and preserved. Some coloured drawings on
their walls are to be seen even now. I have
obtained some views for you from this interesting

* Another name for Alexandropol.

† Ani was one of the first cities and strongest fortresses of the
Armenians, as far back as the second century of our era. In 1064
Alp Arslan took it and massacred the people.

place. The towers and walls are almost intact; but the most extraordinary thing about so large a place is the singular quietness. The country around is perfectly barren, very mountainous, and quite destitute of trees. There are many ruined cities in the neighbourhood, and all dating from about the eleventh century. At that period Ani itself contained 100,000 inhabitants and 500 churches, which shows that more people went to church among them than with us. Before the end of that century it passed into the hands of the Greeks and Saracens. Afterwards the Mongols* took it, and at last an earthquake drove out the remaining inhabitants in 1339; since which time it has been perfectly deserted.

I leave to-morrow for another sixty versts of examination of the frontier. I think there is no doubt of our being able to ascend Ararat,† which is eighty versts distant. The Russian engineers, when they triangulated the Caucasus, lived there for a week. Ararat is 16,953 feet high.‡

The weather is very hot, and the mosquitoes extremely venomous. The conspicuous feature of

---

* In 1239 they captured it, after a short siege, and slaughtered the inhabitants, of whom some had surrendered on a promise of their lives.

† It had been ascended by Parrot in 1829.

‡ Later returns make it 37 feet lower.

the country is beautiful mountain scenery, but for villages and trees one must look in vain. It is quite a desert.

The churches of Ani were built with lava, and crosses of black lava were let in very curiously into the red lava. With the exception of the churches and king's palace, the city is level with the ground; the foundations of the houses being alone discernible. These churches were covered with Armenian inscriptions cut on the walls. I feel myself unable to describe this extraordinary place as it ought to be done. We should have a photographic machine for it. I do not think we shall be very long about the commission, as we have already done a quarter of the whole frontier, 100 versts. The work here is mostly done by us, the Turks looking on. Colonel Simmons does not anticipate being longer than this summer, and I hope it will so turn out. We are now in the province of Erivan, which you remember was taken from Persia in 1829 by Paskievitch. The inhabitants are Persian. We met on our road a great number of Kurds, who live as their fathers did, by travelling about robbing, etc., with their flocks Their children are short of clothing. In spite of the Cossacks, etc., they are as lawless as ever, and go from Turkey to Russia and back again as they like. They are fine-looking people, armed to the teeth, but are decreasing in numbers. They never live in houses, but prefer tents and caves. The number of foxes in these regions is enormous. At Ani itself there are great numbers, and not very wild. There are roebucks also in the mountains. The Russian subjects here are not half so abject as the Moojik or Russian peasant—all of the former carry arms, for instance—and the Government is not so strong as in other parts in putting down robbery, etc. We camp here also, as there are no houses fit to go into, and every day is taken up in surveying and drawing plans without any circumstance occurring worth mentioning. I was never better in health, in spite of mosquitoes, heat, etc. We get up very early, and go to bed the same. We are now on the Aras *—a large river that flows into the Caspian sea. I hope to get a very good map of this country.

Camp, Balikli, July 8, 1857.—Although I cannot fulfil my promise with regard to the description and sketch of Ani just at present, I shall write a line to let you know how I am getting on. I left Hadji Birami the morning after I wrote to

* The ancient Araxes.

you, and had some very hot work the first day; the second day we got into the mountains, and continued on them for the remainder of our labours. We are now scarcely off them, as the level of the lake, on the borders of which we are encamped, is 7430 feet above the sea. It is very deep, and the water very clear and full of fish. During our journey here we were frequently 10,000 feet above the sea. The frontier at this point is to be the watershed separating the waters of the Caspian Sea and Persian Gulf, and our task is to see that the plans supplied by the Russians are correct. My colleagues are one Russian and two Turkish officers. The former is very agreeable, although I cannot talk to him. The Turks are like all Turks. We, James and myself, are attached to different parties, and are small commissioners in our way, as the Turks do nothing, and are quite dependent on our opinion. The scenery from the mountains is splendid, but there is a want of wood which makes the whole country look a desert. Although so extremely hot, there is still snow around us. The nights are cool, and I can assure you that the mosquitoes are most venomous. They howl all night long, and bite in an atrocious manner. They bite horses similarly, having a proboscis as long and sharp as a needle.

M

On the mountains we fell in with the tribes of Kurds, who live at this height during the summer months, quite isolated from the rest of mankind. I paid a visit to the chief of a tribe of 2000. He passed a great number of compliments on the English. This bey is all-powerful with his tribe. He settles all disputes, divides the pasture land among the families, etc. Although living in such a deserted spot they read the Turkish papers, and they asked several questions about the war with Persia,* etc. They are very fanatical, and are much encouraged in their religious fervour by the Sultan's agents. Their houses consist of stone walls covered with camel's hair tents, which are quite water-proof, and lined inside with capital carpets, made by themselves. We encamped near them, and obtained our milk, etc., from them. In order to let us know their habits, they stole the horse of the Russian officer's interpreter during the night. I should not mind trusting them at all, for the Bey would not allow them to take our horses, etc.; perhaps this was only from his hatred to the Russians. Near this Kurdish camp was a mineral spring, excessively cold and strongly impregnated

* That is the English war with Persia, which had just been brought to a successful conclusion.

with carbonic-acid gas. In the small plains near the tops of these mountains there are lots of grass and flowers of every description. We are hard worked, getting up regularly at four a.m. and working until three or four daily; and I must say that to-day is the first since I left Trebizonde that I have had to myself. The atmosphere here is very clear, and everything is perfectly quiet.

In two days we shall leave this to verify the plans as far as Ararat, which now appears pretty close, although fifty versts off. This will take us four days' work. We shall probably stop there four or five days, ascend the mountains, and then shall have finished 220 versts of the frontier, leaving 300 versts to be done. We go back by Erivan to Alexandropol, and from that place work up to the Black Sea. Simmons and Pellissier go to Tiflis for a day or so. I believe there is a chance of the affair ending this year. I cannot make out why it should not, for the territory in dispute is nothing but rock, without either grass or inhabitants. I would not take thirty square miles for a gift, and yet the Turks and Russians cling to it, and get witnesses among the tribes who would swear to anything to support what their respective masters may desire.

The question is where the old frontier between the Persian province of Erivan and the Pashalik of Baizeth was fixed. The Persians ceded the province of Erivan to Paskievitch in 1828; and so now the Russians say the old frontier was in one place, and of course the Turks are not less positive that it was in another; and both sides equally support their contentions with any amount of false swearing. My own belief is that there never was any real frontier between them at all.

The other day we saw a sacred ibis walking majestically along a ridge of snow with its young one. The mother was very much disgusted at being perceived, as there was no chance of concealment on the snow. We caught the young one after a vigorous defence. It was about eighteen inches high, and very strong. The mother appeared greatly delighted at getting its ugly offspring back. They are very tall when full grown, nearly four feet high. I ought to know this frontier pretty well when we have done, as we go over the ground at a foot pace, and with the map examine every feature of it. From Hadji Birami to this we have passed over sixty miles without meeting with a single village. The settlements of the Kurds I have mentioned cannot be called such, as they never remain in one place for any length of time.

Camp, near Mount Ararat, July 22, 1857.—We arrived here on the 19th inst., having left our encampment at Lake Balikli on the 15th. Our road for the first two days was over the ridge which separates the plains of Erivan and Baizeth. This ridge is to be the future frontier.

When we arrived at the foot of Mount Ararat we were unable to proceed along the frontier any further because the ground becomes extremely broken by the innumerable streams of lava which have run down from Mount Ararat. The ground here is black with cinders and every species of volcanic matter, and swarms with scorpions, etc., which have Ararat as their head-quarters. The cinders look as if quite recently emitted, and no one would imagine from their appearance that Ararat had been extinct so long. Our road went along the northern or Russian slope of Mount Ararat, and passed through a very old city called Kourgai, where there are still the remains of a church and part of an old castle. Even the Armenians do not pretend to know its history; but some of them say that Noah lived there. It is situated half-way up the mountain, and there is no living person within twelve miles of it. There used to be a populous village named Aralik, with 5000 inhabitants, a little

above it; but in 1840 an earthquake shook Mount
Ararat, and in four minutes an immense avalanche
had buried this place so completely as to leave
scarcely any vestige of its site. Not a single person
escaped, which is not to be wondered at, considering
the mass that fell. Stones of twenty or thirty tons
were carried as far as fifteen to twenty miles into
the plain. It has left a tremendous cleft in Ararat
itself. Imagine what a weight of snow alone must
have fallen when the Russians measured it at the
top as being 210 feet thick! Other villages were
destroyed at the same time, but none so completely
as this. The village immediately below Aralik
was also destroyed, but the graveyard remained
untouched, and the tombstones stand up intact in
the midst of the ruins. The common people say
that it was saved on account of a saint who was
buried there. All these places have a very lonely
look. A few Kurds, and they only now and then,
pass by the road, as there is no water except at
night. During the day not a drop is to be had.
The cause of this is that the snow which melts
during the day only arrives at night.

The whole country is destitute of trees. There
are, however, quantities of grass, flowers; and a
good many partridges also. The whole country,

with its scorched and uninhabited appearance, has
a very solemn look about it.   Both the Kurds and
the Armenians, if they can possibly help it, never
pass near Mount Ararat, while they think it a great
sin to ascend it.

We are now encamped near the road to Baizeth
from Erivan, between Little and Great Ararat.
Little Ararat is a conical-shaped mountain, and
has a crater on the summit, which, from being
below the limit of perpetual snow, is a small lake.
It is easy of ascent, and I shall try it if I have
time.

I must now tell you of my ascent, or rather very
near ascent, of Great Ararat.   On Monday I and
my interpreter and three sappers went up to a
Kurdish encampment, where an old Kurd lived who
assisted five of our countrymen to ascend about
two years ago.   The only assistance, however, that
he appeared able to give us was to show us where
these Englishmen had encamped the night before
their ascent.   We consequently pitched our tents
there, and settled ourselves for the night.   The
night proved to be very stormy, with thunder and
rain, which was a bad look-out for us.   However,
we started at four a.m. the next morning, and had
some very hard work up to the line of perpetual

snow. My interpreter and two of the sappers gave
it up before this; but I and the other, Corporal
Fisher, held on.

The whole of this time there was a thick fog,
which now and then cleared away, though only for
brief moments, and enabled us to get a splendid
view of the country, spread out as a map beneath
us, with cumuli clouds floating about. The snow
which I mounted was at a very steep slope and
quite hard, nearly ice on the surface. It was so
steep that we could not sit down without holding
on tightly to our poles. Corporal Fisher was about
half a mile to my left, and had a better ascent, as it
was not quite so steep. About two o'clock I began
to get very tired, not able to get up more than two
yards without resting. This was caused by the
rarification of the air. The mist cleared just at this
time for a minute, and I was enabled to see the
summit about 1000 feet above me (but still a further
very steep ascent). Little Ararat was also visible
3000 feet below me. It began to snow soon after
this, and became intensely cold. The two together
settled me, and I turned round, although very
reluctantly, and sitting down, slid over in a very
few minutes the distance which had taken me so
many hours to clamber up. I got back about five
o'clock, and rather tired.

Corporal Fisher managed to get up to the top, and describes the crater to be very shallow, although the top is very large. I expect it was filled with snow. The Kurd told me afterwards that the road I took was very difficult, and that the other English explorers went up a road which was comparatively easy. I believe, however, that if the weather had been more favourable I should have succeeded. The only harm I suffered from my attempt was very sore eyes next day, which Corporal Fisher had also. This was caused by the glare of the snow. Thus ended my unsuccessful attempt. The Russian officer did not want me to go up, and consequently we had no assistance from him. I dare say Simmons will try it when he arrives here.

July 23.—Since writing the above I received orders to join Simmons forty miles from our last camp, which I at once set about doing. I found him encamped some distance from Ararat, in the plain of Erivan. We, that is, myself and James, leave this the day after to-morrow, and proceed with our work to the north of Gumri (about ninety miles from here). Simmons and the commissioners go to Tiflis and rejoin us at Akhaltsikh. This will take us seventeen days, and I really begin to think we shall finish up to the Black Sea in less than two months. Our work is now half finished, and our future labours will be in a very good country, and not half so unhealthy as people make out. I shall write to you from Erivan or Gumri, and let you know any news that may turn up. Simmons will be only accompanied by his secretary, and will only stop at Tiflis eight days. You shall have a sketch of Ani as soon as I have time to do it.

Gumri, August 6, 1857.—I have to acknowledge your letter of June 29, and to thank you for it. Since my last letter I have returned to Gumri, and leave it for good on August 9. I rejoined Simmons and the commissioners soon after I wrote to you, and started with them for Erivan. We passed through the oldest of the Armenian churches and monasteries, a place called Etchmiazin.* It professes to be 1500 years old, and certainly has the appearance of great antiquity ; it was existing during the time of the ruined city of Ani, and

* Etchmiazin is the name of the place where is the convent which provides a residence for the chief Catholicos of the Armenian Church—the Pope, in short, of the Armenian world. The church was built in the first years of the fourth century, by St. Gregory, on a spot where he had seen a vision. It retains its early paramount position at the present time, and the recent election of Mgr. Nersès to the dignity of Catholicos has drawn renewed attention to this place.

is built in a similar style. The relics there are
greatly esteemed. People make pilgrimages to
this monastery from all parts. There is firstly
an arm of St. Gregory, which is enclosed in a
gold case covered with precious stones; next the
piece of the ark, which is necessarily of great
antiquity; a piece of the cross and of the spear,
and a finger-nail of St. Peter, complete the relics.
All these are enveloped in gold cases, and richly
ornamented with every sort of precious stones.
The monastery owns ten villages and a great deal
of land. The monks gave us a grand dinner, and
their feeding certainly was not bad. From this
place we went to Erivan, which is almost in the
same state as when it was taken from the Persians
in 1827, by Paskievitch. There is very little improvement in the town. The fortress is of mud,
and of very little value at present. The Emperor
Nicholas, when he visited it, remarked that Paskievitch had gained his title of Paskievitch Erivanskei
very easily. The fortress was taken by assault
after a seven days' siege.

The palace of the sirdar of the province of Erivan
is beautifully placed, and the colours on the walls
are as fresh as ever, although 100 years old. The
monks' council chamber at Etchmiazin was also

splendidly got up, all the ceiling being carved and gilded. Erivan is so very hot and dusty during the summer that all the employés of the Government leave it for the mountains. All the inhabitants are Persian, and wear the Persian costume. The town is prettily situated, and has large gardens around it. In the fortress we saw the four howitzers which were taken from the Turks at Schwinjel, and eleven more that were taken at Bachkileclaire. The Turkish commissioners did not like the sight much, as you may imagine.

We stayed at Erivan two days, and then started to rejoin our caravan, which had proceeded on the road to Gumri. Simmons left us on the second day with his secretary. We overtook our baggage at the base of the mountain I have previously mentioned—Alagos,* 13,480 feet above the sea. As we had to stop here two days to allow Colonel Pellissier, the French commissioner, who is unwell, to rejoin us, we decided to try the ascent; so the day after our arrival we started with some Kurdish guides to the mountain, and, after a good deal of delay, got to the place where the only path to the summit commences. Here we were obliged to dis-

---

* This means "the Motley Mount," called so from the various colours it presents.

mount and take to our legs. After about two and a half hours we got to the summit, and were extremely glad of it, for although it is not to be compared to Mount Ararat, it is still rather difficult. We boiled some water on the top, to ascertain the height, and then descended. Trusting to my Ararat experience, I thought of descending on the snow, and started. I was much astonished at finding the slope far steeper than I expected, and consequently went down like a shot, and reached the bottom one hour and a half before the others. A Russian doctor tried it after me, and in trying to change his direction was turned round, and went to the bottom, sometimes head foremost. He was not a bit hurt. The distance we slid down in two minutes or less was upwards of 3000 feet. There was no danger, as we had only to keep ourselves straight. My trousers are the only sufferers !

We were extremely lucky in getting up so well, as the Russian general who triangulated the Caucasus was three weeks encamped at the base before he could ascend, and then he only managed it once. He lost one man during his ascent by lightning. The ground about is covered with stone containing sulphur, and sometimes you can find the pure yellow crystals. We saw a white bear and two cubs close to the mountain.

I was the first up, our doctor, Woodfall, next, then James, and Jones, and a Cossack. None of the Russians succeeded. We managed to get back to camp through a very rocky country by eleven p.m. There happened to be close to our encampment the chief of the Russian Kurds, Jaffer Agha. He asked us to dinner, which we accepted. He is a very powerful man, and the Russians are very anxious to retain his friendship, as it must always prove of the greatest use during war. In the last campaign he kept all the Turkish Kurds quiet by means of bribes, etc., and prevented them from pillaging. He was present at the coronation of the emperor, and has received a great many rings, snuff-boxes, etc., and also the crosses of St. Anne and Stanislas. The Russians, although they have possessed this country for thirty years, do not appear to have established themselves very securely in it, and certainly do not make the progress they ought. Although the plain of Erivan is very rich, the Government gains no revenue from it, but sends money every year from St. Petersburg. I suspect the employés are great rascals. From all I can hear, they are able to pillage with impunity, for it is very seldom any one comes this way who has power to make known all their misdeeds.

We arrived here on the 6th, and I shall leave
on the 9th. I expect that the commission will be
finished in six weeks, and that by the end of
October we shall be near England. I am uncertain
how I shall come home. My principal object in
wishing to be in England is to try if I can get into
the staff corps. Otherwise I should be very well
contented with this, although not very remunera-
tive in a pecuniary sense.

Akhaltsikh, Aug. 21, 1857.—It is some time since
I wrote to you, but my excuse must be that I have
been very much engaged during the last fortnight.
We are, however, now settled here for two or three
days, and have only 100 versts (about seventy
miles) more of the frontier to go over. This will
probably take a fortnight; after which we may
expect another fortnight's delay to finish up our
work, and then we shall return home, I hope,
about the end of October. Our work, since Gumri,
has been over some very fine mountainous country,
the latter part of it a good deal wooded. We found
a large colony of the Daghoboortz, a sect something
like the Mormons, who were transported to the
number of 2000 souls, into this country out of
Russia in 1840. They are fine-looking people, and

have very good villages. We have had a bad accident with one of the sappers, who was out shooting
and fell down; the gun went off, and shot him in
the leg. The wound is going on well, but the man
will have to be left here some time in the Russian
hospital. I am going up the country from here for
two days, and when I return I start for my destination in the Adjar country. This country, which
is inhabited by a tribe of Lazes, has not been
visited by many Europeans or even Russians.
During our last journey, every field of maize, etc.,
had little sheds, where the owner remained all
night to watch against the Lazes and bears, both
of which commit great devastation occasionally.
Akhaltsikh is a very pretty town with 14,000 inhabitants. It was taken after a siege by Paskievitch
in 1829, and several very severe actions were fought
in the neighbourhood. The Russians still keep
up the citadel and have a considerable garrison
there. I expect to be able to pay a visit to Kutais
and perhaps Tiflis before my departure. Kutais is
the capital of Imeritia, and the princess who
governs is called independent of Russia, but it is
probable that it will be taken entirely by Russia
very soon, as they have got up a revolution among
the peasants, and after it is put down they will

make an investigation, and declare that the present government is bad, pension the princess, and annex the country. I leave this to-morrow, and will write again before I leave this country to let you know when we may be expected home ; but I think that this letter will be very nearly the last you will receive. I could write more, but that I am very much engaged getting ready for my departure.

Constantinople, Sept. 28, 1857.—I am sure you will be astonished at seeing that we have arrived here, having finished all our work, as you will not have received any letters for some time. The reason is that since my last visit to Gumri and the present time, only one mail has left us for England, partly from the country on the side of Turkey being so unsafe that we could not send couriers, and also because we could not send the mail except by a very long roundabout way. I have to acknowledge two letters from ——, and two from you, your last being received to-day, dated September 15. All these came nearly the same time. I am extremely distressed to hear of poor Willie Anderson's death, and every one who knew him will be so. He was a sterling good comrade and officer, greatly liked by both officers and men, and our corps has sustained a great loss in him. I am

N

so very sorry for poor dear ——, it is such a
sudden blow to her, and I am sure they must have
been so happy together during their short married
life.

I expect to be in England (D.V.) in about a fortnight, as our work is now finished. I will not
give you any history of my past travels until I see
you, beyond telling you that after leaving Gumri
we proceeded northward, and got on very well up
to Akhalkalak, where we rejoined the commissioners, who had been to Tiflis (that place was
taken by Paskievitch by assault in 1829). From
there we proceeded along the frontier to near
Akhaltsikh, where the commissioners assembled.
This we found to be a very nice place. It was
defended for some time against Paskievitch, in 1829,
by the Lazes, a warlike set of people who inhabit
Lazistan. He fought three actions here, and eventually took the town and castle by assault, losing a
great many men. The Turks pushed forward to this
place during the war, but were afraid to attack it.
The Russians got some troops together while they
were hesitating, and attacked them in a fog, de-
feated them, and took nineteen guns. At this
place the commissioners separated. Simmons went
on a tour, and the others rejoined him at Kutais,

capital of Imeritia. James and myself went, as usual, along the frontier. I had eighty versts of frontier where not many Europeans had been before. On one side of it was Lazistan, and this part of Lazistan is peopled by the fiercest tribe of Lazes, who scarcely acknowledge even the Sultan. We had an escort of forty infantry, and were not molested. This tribe and the Kabouletians supply the Constantinople Turks with slaves, whom they kidnap from the Gourelians, who are on the Russian side. These Gourelians are beautiful; in fact, generally speaking, I never saw so many handsome men and women as the peasants among them. The Adjars are most daring, and even proposed to us to bring any person we might choose out to Batoum for £40 to £120. In consequence of these kidnappings, etc., a deadly enmity exists between the two peoples, and whenever they get a chance they kill one another. During the last eighteen months sixty-two people have been kidnapped, sixteen killed, and twenty or thirty wounded on the part of the Gourelians. The Russian guards of the frontier are futile against these people, for the latter are armed with a capital rifle, and are also splendid shots, while the Cossacks have only a trumpery smooth-bore.

The country of the Adjars is very mountainous
indeed, and quite impracticable except on foot,
being covered with dense forests. Gouriel, on the
contrary, is quite flat, but covered also with forests.
These valleys are " the deadly swamps," according
to some people. I dare say they are not very
healthy, but they are not so bad as made out.
There are numerous rivers, and consequently plenty
of swamps also. It is the most splendid country in
the world for luxuriant vegetation. I assure you
we saw wild fig-trees, pears, apples, grapes, hops,
rhododendrons, azalias, and laurels growing in the
most luxuriant manner. The wild pears were
magnificent, very large, and yet nobody thought
it worth while to gather them. The above are
dispersed generally throughout the whole of the
provinces. The tangle of hops and grape vine
on some trees was enough to strangle anything.

I must qualify my remark about the healthiness
of this region. Some localities, I find, are very unhealthy. A space of twenty versts—about fourteen
miles—requires as a guard of frontier a squadron of
Cossacks. The Russian general told us that every
year there were 150 men died from fever out of
this guard alone. The Russians never say over the
mark, so you can imagine what the sickness must

be. I forgot to tell you that the army of the Caucasus, consisting of 150,000 men, dies out completely in five years. This is known from the fact that every year 30,000 men (recruits) are marched into the Caucasus and never a body of 1000 march out. Each regiment stays 25 years in the Caucasus. The Government of the Caucasus brings in no revenue, but every year receives large sums from St. Petersburgh. All the *employés* and officers thieve right and left, and the poor soldiers suffer in consequence. After a short stay at Kutais, the commissioners rejoined James and myself at Ozurgeth, the capital of Gouriel, and after a stay of ten days there, we agreed that it would be better to resume the deliberations at Constantinople; so Mons. Pellissier and our party started for Batoum (a beastly place, where every one looks dying of fever), where we met a steamer which took us down here, after a tolerable passage. I cannot say exactly when I shall be with you, but expect about the middle of the month of October. I will let you know before I start. There is no news here.

Constantinople, Oct. 7, 1857.—I have not left this place yet, but expect to do so on the 10th inst. The cause of my delay has been a great deal on account of Colonel Simmons and three others of our party being ill. They have, however, now got over the worst part, and are recovering. All our party had been perfectly well during the whole time we were in Asia, but the change of air on arriving here produced (on the above) a very bad bilious attack. The French commissioner and his servants are also laid up with the same thing. I am, I am happy to say, in capital health, and hope to find you all well, when I arrive.

P.S.—My surveying duties have been usurped by those of sick nurse, etc.

Greenhythe, April 24, 1858.*—We start at two p.m. I will write from Gibraltar. I expect the vessel will take twenty days before she arrives at Constantinople.

Havre, April 26, 1858.—We arrived last night after a good passage; but I must say the accommodation is not of the very best description. We shall not get to Constantinople until May 14, so do not expect to hear from me until that time. The passengers are not very select, but are amusing. A good many began boldly in the

* General Gordon had passed the winter of 1857–58 in England.

feeding line, but it was no good; bacon will not
remain on the stomach. We have two babies who
are very musical at times, one of which has the
whooping cough, and it is interesting to remark
how long it will be before the other catches it.
There was a very lively young lady, with bird-
like motions, a volatile being, who however dis-
appeared when we began rolling, and did not
appear again until we arrived here. She is very
fascinating. Our doctor discovered the reason of
the babies being quiet up to yesterday. He
found a paper entitled " —— Soothing Powders "
lying on the deck, and which we presume was
given to the children. It contains nothing but
opium. We came just in time to-day to see a
swell marriage take place; the bride seemed to
take it very coolly. I was very foolish not going
overland, which I might have done.

Malta, May 10, 1858.—You will be surprised to
find that we have not yet arrived at Constantinople; but it almost seems as if our voyage was
a yachting excursion, we have taken so long
about it. We were told in a loose way by the
captain that we should leave Havre on the Wed-
nesday morning after we arrived, so Woodfall and

myself slept on shore on Tuesday night (as we anticipated enjoying the pleasures of the ship quite long enough during the voyage out). About ten o'clock we sauntered down to the wharf, and did not find the vessel. It did not trouble us much, and we proceeded to the entrance of the harbour, expecting she had laid to there. When we got to the entrance we found her waiting for us, and on our arrival she attempted to pass out, but found the tide had left her on the mud. This, of course, delayed us twelve hours, and was entirely the fault of the pilot, in not having laid to outside. I enclose a scrap of the Havre *Gazette* which relates to our mishap. In any other vessel but this it would have been annoying; but, as I said before, time seems no object to us. The vessel is pretty steady, which she ought to be considering she goes only about nine knots per hour. We had a very disagreeable passage across the Bay and passed Gibraltar on May 5, not stopping, although I had a parcel and letter for ——, and which I had volunteered taking out. It is very unfortunate, and will oblige me to send it back from this place. The passengers consist of Mr. ——, his wife, and a sister of his; the latter is a fairy-like young lady who makes the most correct remarks, and would come under the denomination of a very nice, agreeable person. There is a Mr. ——, who was invisible during the former part of the voyage, but now makes up for lost time in the eating line. Mr. ——, a stately individual who is to make the stations, etc., of the line, and who is dignity itself. These, with two clerks, compose the staff of the Smyrna Railway Company. The captain has his wife with him, and a small baby, who is at present suffering from whooping cough, and is correspondingly agreeable. We anxiously watched if ——'s children would take it; but as yet they have not. The above-mentioned baby, with ——'s, proclaim the dawn by a concert every morning, caused, I suppose, by the ablutions. I shall write from Constantinople, and perhaps add a few lines to this, which, in spite of its date, is written on board the *Bellona* (our steam vessel, which I do not recommend to any one with whom time is an object).

Constantinople, May 17, 1858.—Many thanks for your note, which I received on my arrival here yesterday. . . . We only stopped twelve hours at Malta, where I saw many old friends, and then went on to Smyrna, where we got rid of the engineers, etc., of the railway. This railway is now only five miles in length, but when finished is to extend to Aidin, a town in the interior, seventy miles from the sea. It will take four years to finish it, and the estimated cost is £1,200,000. They find it very difficult to teach the natives blasting, as they have no sense of caution. One of them lost his life the other day by jamming the borer into the hole, when half filled with powder ; it ignited and removed his head.

Smyrna is decidedly the best town of the Levant. It is tolerably clean, and well situated. We stopped only twelve hours, and then proceeded to Constantinople (thirty-six hours distant). I found James had arrived three days before ; but as it was the Bairam feast we could do nothing until to-day. I saw Alison this morning, with James ; he is at present *chargé d'affaires* until Sir H. Bulwer * arrives. He was dressed out in a very Oriental style, and received us affably. To-morrow we shall pay our visit to the Porte and the Russian Embassy. I expect we shall be here for another six days. Ivan is well ; but he never is unwell.

* The late Lord Dalling.

May 18.—We have just seen the Russian minister, who was very civil. I think it likely that I shall go by Odessa and the Crimea to Redout Kaleh. I enclose a panorama of Constantinople for my father.

Constantinople, May 26, 1858.—I leave this day for Redout Kaleh *viâ* Odessa, Sebastopol, and Kertch, and expect to arrive about June 5.

Redout Kaleh, June 3, 1858.—I write in haste to tell you that I have arrived safe at the above place, having left Constantinople on the 26th ult., and finding, on my arrival on the 28th at Odessa, a small steamer called the *Akermann*, thirty-five horse-power, about to start for Redout Kaleh, I determined to go in her, as I had missed the regular packet by twenty-four hours, and should have had to wait a fortnight for the next. I consequently started on Saturday, May 29 ; arrived at Sebastopol on the 30th, and remained there twenty-four hours. The town is still an utter ruin; scarcely anything has been done to restore it. The grass has so overgrown the place where the camps stood that it was with difficulty I found my hut. The graveyards are well cared for, but covered with grass. About 8000 or 9000 people are in the town. They are miserably poor, and most of them live in the cellars of the houses. Some wooden huts have also been erected in the streets; but, generally speaking, the place is deserted, and looks very gloomy. The Russian works and our trenches have subsided into insignificant heaps, and give no idea of their original size. I thought we had dug up every root, but at present small oak bushes about fifteen inches high are springing up everywhere, and in five years more the ground will be scarcely known again.

Redout Kaleh, June 5, 1858.—I shall send a few lines before my departure for Kutais, where I expect to meet my Russian colleague. My camp here is on the sea-shore, in a capital position. The mountains of the Caucasus, covered with snow, extend to the north for some distance, and they present a superb appearance. The whole country is beautifully wooded, and only requires draining to be a delightful place of residence, as there is scarcely any winter, and the heat is not unbearable in summer. You must not be put out if my letters come in a shoal, with long intervals between, as the postal arrangements are not over good. I shall send this off at once.

Ozurgeth, June 16.—I left Redout Kaleh on June 10, having heard from General Miliutine, the chef d'état major of the governor-general, that my Russian colleague, Ogranovitch, had just left Kutais for Ozurgeth. After two days' hard marching we arrived at the latter place, where we met with my old companion. The Turkish officer has not yet turned up, but we expect him daily. The waiting here is very annoying, as I have nothing to do, and so can have little to say. A great many old acquaintances came to pay me visits, and are very civil. Ivan and all the party are well, although here it is rather hot. Our escort when we do move is to be fifty Russian infantry, and 250 Turkish ditto.

Ozurgeth, June 29, 1858.—Still at the same place and without the Turk. I have been to Kutais for a day or so. It is a very decent town for these parts, and beautifully situated on the river Rion (the ancient Phasis). I dined with the governor-general, Prince Eristaw, who left the next day for Swaneti to overawe the subjects of the late Prince (he was shot at Kutais for stabbing Prince Gagarin, the predecessor of Prince Eristaw), who do not seem to have relished his death. The prince

takes two battalions of infantry and two guns,
nominally as an escort. I shall watch with great
interest his career, as they seem to think there will
be some hard fighting if the Russians do not win
the people over by money and promises. You will
find Swaneti to the N.W. of Kutais in the map.
The people wear the enclosed patch on their heads,
allowing the hair to be very long. The Mingrelians,
Imeritians, and Gourelians used to wear their
caps of the same size ; however, the three last-named
people did not find it sufficient, and so enlarged it
to the size I brought home. This form seems to be
derived from the shape of a sling, with which in
ancient times they were very expert. You shall
have a fuller history of all these people in my next
note.

I am sorry to say that they have not succeeded in
the navigation of the Rion river up to the present.
This river, having its source in the snows of the
Caucasus range, is of course liable to sudden rises
and falls. The small steamer which transported me
to Redout Kaleh from Odessa is now prevented
from descending, and will have to remain in her
present position for probably the whole summer.
The Russians do not understand how to work these
affairs. Their idea is to get the trade from Persia

(which now passes through Bayazid, Erzeroum, and Trebizonde) to pass by the Caspian Sea to the mouth of the Aras river, then up that river, and the river Kur, which is navigable to a place called Mintgitschawi, to Marau or Ust Tchenis Tchala, on the river Rion (and where it commences to be navigable) by a proposed railway through Tiflis, Gori, Suram, and Sharopan. Being at first in a great hurry to do this, they sent for two steamers to work on the river Rion (from Marau or Ust Tchenis Tchala to Poti, at the entrance of the river Rion). Having made a reconnaissance only of that river, and not having taken a regular set of soundings for the whole year, which is necessary in order to understand the greatest fall to which it is liable, the consequence is, that they must now send for a dredging-machine, and, letting these steamers remain idle, clear the river sufficiently to allow them to pass out.

Poti is intended to be a very large town, but at present they have not got further than being occupied in cutting down the forest. The inhabitants of Trebizonde, Erzeroum, and along the caravan road have taken the alarm, on hearing of the arrival of the steamers on the Rion, and are trying hard to get a good road or railway made, so as to keep the trade in their hands. The Russians have thus put the Turks and ourselves on guard, and it is to be hoped that something will be done to prevent the two million pounds worth of English goods which pass annually by the caravan road from Trebizonde, being at the mercy of the Russians. The weather here is very hot, but the evenings are delightful. Fireflies and jackals abound, and nightingales also. Duke,* Ivan, and all the party are well. There are some very pretty ladies at Kutais, who dance their national dances capitally. As I told you, they dance alone, and all the gentlemen beat time with their hands. I intend going to Ludidi, in Mingrelia, near where the battle of Tugour was fought, and seeing that part of the country. You can hardly conceive the magnificent views there are about the Caucasus. They say that coal, lead, and silver abound there. I was surprised at seeing the ladies wear a sort of bracelet of black beads, and to which they attached great value. When at Kutais I made inquiry, and found that they could be only procured at one place near Kutais, each bead being made by hand. I examined them, and am sure they are nothing more than bog-oak. I send you some of them. The frontier I shall not touch on at

* The name of a dog.

present, as it will be time enough to say something when we begin our operations. The Grand Dukes Michael and Nicholas are coming here in September, and great preparations are being made for their reception. I must now conclude, hoping —— has got over his wound.

Ozurgeth, June 29, 1858.—Many thanks for your note, if two sheets can be called a note. The ladies are very pretty, but have not very cleanly habits, in general; they prefer their nails tipped, and do not hesitate at taking a bone and gnawing it. They live in extremely dirty houses, or rather, huts. They are generally all princesses, and the men all princes, who, however, do not hesitate to accept small donations. I am always in fear and trembling lest they should give me anything, as it is necessary to give in return (——'s notion; as I told him, he has several Eastern habits). I unfortunately happened to notice a certain glass letter-weight, with the Queen on it, and observed that it was like her Majesty; I was given it on the spot, and with deep regret had to part with my soda-water machine the next day. I admire nothing now, you may be sure. The servants of Prince Dimitri Gouriel have made a good thing out of my visit, for each time they bring anything—butter, fruit,

O

etc.—orders are given that an equivalent be given
them in money. My hands get quite sticky with
shaking hands with so many princes; but I have
hitherto borne up like a martyr under my trials.
On being invited to the house of a prince, you
would figure yourself invited to a palace, but it is
not the case here, and you would find it out, to
your cost, if you did not take something to eat in
your pockets. . . . I declare I think Ivan has a
liking for Emma. The enclosed, in Russian, is for
the whole of the servants from him. However, I
do not mean to allow it, as he belongs to me.
I have found out that he is a Lutheran, and reads
his Bible regularly.

Tcholok River, eight miles from Ozurgeth, July
19, 1858.—I am glad to announce to you the commencement of our work. The Turk, Yarif Bey,
and two aide-de-camps, arrived on the 12th inst.,
with 260 soldiers, and we have begun cutting down
the wood, which abounds in these parts. We are
only able, however, to cut down a narrow strip
along the frontier, of nine yards, in order to mark
it out to the local authorities, who will have to cut
down upwards of 200 yards, so as to establish the
proper posts along the line. I imagine we shall

remain here ten days, and after that time proceed through Adjara to the mountains, which will be a great advantage, as these plains are not very healthy.   Up to the present, however, we have all been well.   I received a letter from you, dated June 16.   The beads I sent you last time were made of *cannel coal*, not bog oak.   I like your idea of old one-legged Mr. —— being appointed to any place away from the Foreign Office.   He has been there fifty years, and will remain always, until he leaves for good.   —— is a very hopeful correspondent; his last letter had five "hopes" in it, and three or four "I am sures."   We are undergoing a gentle drizzling rain, which has continued nearly all day, and which is disagreeable in tents, and not very convenient for the kitchen.   We shall finish by the month of October, I think, and afterwards I intend, if possible, paying a visit to Tiflis. There are quantities of wild boar here, but I have shot nothing of late.   Close to our present camp, a battle was fought, in 1855, between the Turks and Russians; the latter gained the victory, and took fourteen guns.

Mount Solimérie, near Akhaltsikh, Aug. 17, 1858.
—I almost forget the date of my last letter, but my

having been so much engaged must be my excuse. You will be glad to hear that we have finished the first half of our work, and may expect to complete it some time in October. I made an excursion from the frontier into Kula, the chief village of Adjara, and where I do not believe any Englishman has yet been. It is, however, a miserable place, and not worth the trouble of getting there. Nothing whatever remarkable is to be seen in it. While in the place we heard that a Russian deserter was going to be sold. It is a hard lot for them, after they have effected their escape from the Russian army, to be sold as slaves.

I assure you the work we have had to do has been most fatiguing, it being quite impossible to go on horseback. We have cut through forest for nearly eight miles, where not even a road passes at present. We are pretty well past the worst part, and will soon arrive in more civilized regions. I have not received a post for some time, but cannot expect to get letters when our best road to the plain is by an alley cut in the wood by ourselves. I expect to stop a few days on the Poschouchai river, and intend visiting Akhaltsikh from there. We are now near the Koblian Tchai river. Prince Bariatinski, the governor-general of the Caucasus, is there, and is

anxious to see us. You must know that we are
the third commission which has endeavoured to
arrange this frontier, all the others having been
obliged to give it up on account of the difficulties. I
do not complain when there is no occasion, but really
this work has been most fatiguing. My Turkish
colleague, a stupid fellow, has just had an attack of
fever, which will not tend to hasten our work; but
now we are on the mountains I do not care if we
are delayed a few days, as it is very healthy, and
the scenery is magnificent. You really must excuse
my writing, as it is very cold, and the time I can
spare is very short. My work consists chiefly in
arranging the affairs of my two colleagues; such
as finding the pyramids we placed last year on the
frontier, and which the inhabitants have carefully
destroyed; finding out the line to be cut in the
woods, etc.; and in generally keeping the two
others from squabbling. Having received no letters
for more than a month, I can answer no questions;
and as my life is more the work of an animal than
anything else, I cannot amuse you much. Our
chief griefs are in our animals of transport, and in
the bad roads which prevent our tents, etc., arriving
until very late every day, and which cause an
immense amount of anxiety as to whether they

will arrive at all, as it happens sometimes that two or three of my horses are left behind, and on one occasion, my personal luggage, which was on a mule, fell down a precipice, and the mule was killed, but my traps were not much the worse. I will endeavour to write a longer and more detailed letter in a day or two, after my visit to Akhaltsikh.

Korzapine Göl or Lake, Sept. 10, 1858.—We are now encamped on the above lake, and are within forty miles of our destination, namely, the source of the Arpatchai river, and the place where our work finishes. It will, however, be at least a fortnight before we arrive there. I think I mentioned that the Russians had established four days' quarantine for people coming from Turkey. This prevents me at least from passing into their territory, as I have no idea of undergoing the four days. I visited Akhaltsikh for an hour or so, but found the place so dull and hot that I returned very soon to my camp. Since my last letter we have not done much beyond replacing the temporary boundary marks I erected last year by stone pyramids. The Turk, Yarif Bey, has been ill ever since he left the Koblian river, although the climate is excellent. I expect there is a little shamming in it. The Russian commissioner and he are always bickering about trifles, and I am pretty tired of my post of peacemaker, for which I am naturally not well adapted. However, as yet things have gone on well between them. The grand dukes are expected in three or four days. They pass close to this *en route* to Alexandropol, and I dare say we shall see them. Our life is very monotonous. The lake near which we are encamped has existed only forty years, and there are several islands with ruined villages on them which the old inhabitants of these parts remember to have been accessible from the mainland. There always existed a marsh, but about forty years ago a small spring broke out in the same, which eventually spread over the marsh and formed this lake. It is about 1500 feet higher than the bed of the river Kura, and only distant four miles from the latter river. The inhabitants have constructed a small canal from the lake to the Kura. I should like to see this deepened and the lake let out into the Kura. It would carry away all the Russian bridges as far as the Caspian Sea. I hear nothing whatever of James, and cannot make out what he is about. It is two months since I had a letter from him. The last I received from you was dated July 14, and was

received at the same time as Rarey's book, for
which I am much obliged. I am very glad to hear
that Bayly has got over his wound so well, and
would willingly exchange with Enderby, although
I think the Indian affairs are nearly at an end, and
we may occupy ourselves in the reorganization of
the country. The four companies to be added to
our corps make no difference to me, as there are no
officers to be appointed. If the roads are not im-
passable by the snow you may expect us about
December. I am quite in the dark as to how my
mission has been fulfilled, but it is really immaterial
to me, for I will not accept other work of such an
anomalous character. I have had capital health
throughout the commission, and that although we
stopped six weeks in the marshes of Gouriel. I
had only one slight attack of fever, which I speedily
cured. I have been to Ardahan since I wrote, and
was very much pleased with my visit. It is well
situated, and, if the Russians had not burnt most of
the houses during the war, would be a flourishing
city. The mudir, or magistrate of the district
received me very well, and it is curious to see the
confidence they have in the English. They speak
of us as their true friends, and you never hear the
name of France pronounced. I have just heard

from James, who has also nearly finished his work, and expects to join me in ten days. We are now encamped near Lake Tchylder, close to the village of Chandra. There have been some disturbances in these districts, owing to the Porte wishing to take the inhabitants as soldiers. These latter threatened, if they were taken, that the remainder would pass into the Russian territory. The consequence is that they have been let off for this year. We had a severe frost the day before yesterday, and the mountains around were covered with snow. The inhabitants say that winter will commence in about three weeks' time. I am afraid you will say I have very little to tell you; but our life is very monotonous, and there is very little to interest you. The Russians gave a spread (vulgar) on Saturday, the fête day of their emperor, noisily and badly got up. Their wine was simply execrable. However, they and the Turks got very well over it, and it concluded in the Cossacks tossing the latter, which they did not at all appreciate. I must confess, stupid and conceited as the Turks are, I prefer them to their *apparently more* civilized neighbours. The inhabitants (Mussulman) of the Russian territory frequently come to me and ask me if it is possible to pass them into the Turkish territory. I never met men looking so miserable as these people, who are to be made to pay the expenses of the visit of the grand dukes. These expenses will be great, no doubt; but the inhabitants will have to pay the amount twice over, in order to supply the smaller authorities, who rejoice at this great chance of robbing the peasants. The chief of the district of Ozurgeth is a man who has absolute power over nearly all Gouriel, a district of eighty miles by forty miles. He has no education whatever, is daily tipsy, and is utterly unfit for the smallest employment with us. His pay is £160 per annum; consequently he is obliged to take bribes, etc., in order to live, and this is the case with most of the *employés* of the Caucasus, and accounts for the little hold Russia has over these provinces which she has possessed for fifty years.

Alexandropol, Oct. 4, 1858.—It is a long time since I heard from you, but suppose my letters are wandering about somewhere. You will be glad to hear that we have finished our work, and that we are now preparing for our start home, by Ardahan and Artvin to Batoum, and from thence to Constantinople. This will take us at least a fortnight, during which time you will have no letters. Since I last wrote we have spent a very uninteresting time, and I am very glad that the affair is quietly finished. I met James here on September 24. He has taken several photographs, but finds it difficult to print them here, so we have decided to leave that until our arrival in England. Some of those he had already printed I enclose; you will find the names of these on the backs. The negatives are not bad, and will be very interesting. James's party are all well. The grand dukes passed close to our camp on their way to Alexandropol, but did not stop; their visit was very short (only twelve hours) to this place, when they left for Tiflis. James, although in the town, did not see them. We are going to Tiflis for two or three days, and then return, *viâ* Kars, so as to take some photographs of that place. The others were taken when James was on his way to Ararat, and were not very good. My Turkish colleague goes to Kars at once, as he has been suffering from fever for a long time. I was very lucky in my colleagues, as James was very badly placed, and in consequence had some squabbles which have been referred to by the Home Government. This is chiefly owing to the intrigues of the Turks. You need say nothing about it. The weather was excessively cold about ten days ago, but it has now changed, and is not unseasonable. The frost was so severe as to break bottles in our tents. I hope to be able to get you some mementoes from Tiflis, for as yet I have got nothing.

Constantinople, Nov. 17, 1858.—I arrived here with James last night, after a precious rough voyage from Trebizonde. I think I wrote to you last from Alexandropol, prior to my trip to Tiflis. I received a letter from you while at Kars, and your last I got on my arrival here. I am sorry to think that there is a mail of mine missing in that land of infamous arrangements, viz. holy Russia, which I shall never recover I am afraid. We had a splendid journey from Kars to Ardahan, Ardanuch, and Artvin. The scenery is the finest I ever saw. From Artvin we descended the Tchorok river in caiques, which are splendidly managed by the boatmen, in places where it seems almost impossible for boats to pass. All the details of my visit to Tiflis and of this journey I must leave until I have the pleasure of seeing you, as you may imagine I am very busy, and have a great many things to settle before I leave this, which will probably be in about a week. We have secured some decent photographs, and were lucky enough to get three good views of Kars; but our man is not so apt as he ought to be. Did you ever get the photographs I sent you from this place of Stamboul, etc.? I have never heard them mentioned, also a cap I sent from Gouriel. If you did not get the photographs, I cannot make out what has become of them. I do not feel at all inclined to settle in England and be employed in any sedentary way, and shall try and get employed here if it is possible, intending, however, to return to England first. Do you see how I am creeping up the list of lieutenants? The number of steps we have had lately is extraordinary. I heard from Simmons the other day at Warsaw; he was still suffering from fever and ague. He likes Warsaw, and wants me to pay him a visit. I saw Biddulph yesterday. He is engaged on the Euphrates telegraph, and has done about twenty or thirty miles. You must now excuse me, for I have three or four affairs to settle, and the mail leaves at one p.m. With sincere hope that I shall find you all well, and I will write before my departure from this.

THE END.

PRINTED BY WILLIAM CLOWES AND SONS, LIMITED,
LONDON AND BECCLES.